Greek and Roman Civilizations

BY
Heidi M. C. Dierckx, Ph.D.

COPYRIGHT © 1996 Mark Twain Media, Inc.
ISBN 1-58037-063-2
Printing No. CD–1888

Mark Twain Media, Inc., Publishers
Distributed by Carson-Dellosa Publishing Company, Inc.

TABLE OF CONTENTS

INTRODUCTION

**"NESCIRE AUTEM, QUID ANTEA, QUAM NATUS SIS,
ACCIDERIT, ID EST SEMPER ESSE PUERUM"
CICERO (ORATIONS, 34)**

**"NOT TO KNOW WHAT HAPPENED BEFORE
ONE WAS BORN, IS ALWAYS TO BE A CHILD."**

Western civilization owes much to the Greek and Roman civilizations, which laid the foundation for civilization in the Western world. First came the Greeks who developed an advanced civilization in the Mediterranean. They adopted an alphabet similar to the one we use today. In addition, Greek influence can be seen today in the areas of science, philosophy, literature, theater, art, and architecture. Democracy was also first developed in Greece. The Greeks left behind a legacy inherited by the Romans and still felt in the Western world of today. The Romans were influenced greatly by Greek culture and adopted many of its elements, such as the alphabet, literature, science, art, and architecture. Roman civilization, however, was also influenced by the Etruscan civilization in areas such as predicting the future, elements of government, and architecture. The Romans did not merely copy Greek and Etruscan cultures, but developed a civilization that became distinctly their own, producing their own identity. They contributed the Latin language, which was the basis for the Romance (French, Italian, and Spanish) languages, to the Western world. The Roman Republic type of government was an important model for the government of the United States. Another important Roman legacy to western civilization was the development and spread of Christianity, which today is the most widely-practiced religion in the world. In order to understand our world today, it is necessary to study the impact of the Greek and Roman civilizations of the past.

**"Fair Greece! sad relic of departed worth!
Immortal, though no more! though fallen, great!"**

[Lord Byron, "Childe Harold's Pilgrimage" (1812–1818), canto 2, stanza 73]

GREEK AND ROMAN TIME LINES

DATES IN GREEK HISTORY

ALL DATES B.C.

c. 3000	Beginning of Minoan civilization on Crete
c. 2000–1450	Palace period: building of palaces at Knossos and other places
c. 1450	Destruction of palaces: end of Minoan power
	Volcanic eruption of Thera
c. 1400–1200	Height of Mycenaean civilization: building of palaces at Mycenae and other places
c. 1220 (?)	Trojan War (?)
c. 1200–1150	Destruction of Mycenaean palaces
	Dorian Invasion (?)
c. 1200–750	Dark Age
	Introduction of iron
c. 1050–950	Ionian Migrations
c. 750	Start of Hellenic civilization: rise of city-states, introduction of alphabet, trade increases
776	Traditional date for the first Olympic Games
750–600	Greek colonization
650–500	Rise of tyrannies
594	Solon starts the process of democracy in Athens
560–527	Reign of Peisistratus of Athens
546	Cyrus, king of Persia, conquers Asia Minor, including the Asiatic Greeks
508–507	Cleisthenes' reforms in Athens
by 500	Foundation of Peloponnesian League
499–494	Ionian Revolt
490–479	Persian Wars
490	Persian invasion of Greece under King Darius
	Battle of Marathon
483	Themistocles builds new Athenian fleet
480	King Xerxes invades Greece
	Battle of Thermopylae
	Battle of Salamis
479	Battle of Plataea
	Battle of Mycale
478	Foundation of Delian League
468	Final defeat of Persians at Battle of Euremedon (Asia Minor)
461–429	Rule of Pericles in Athens
431–421	Peloponnesian War I
415–404	Peloponnesian War II
411	Oligarchic Revolution in Athens
405	Battle of Aegospotami: defeat of Athens
404–403	Rule of the Thirty Tyrants in Athens

404–371	Supremacy of Sparta
386	King's Peace
371	Battle of Leuctra: Theban victory
371–362	Supremacy of Thebes; rule of Epaminondas at Thebes
362	Battle of Mantinea: Spartan and Athenian victory
359–336	Rule of Philip II of Macedonia
338	Battle of Chaeronea: Philip II conquers the Greeks
336–323	Rule of Alexander the Great
336–30	Hellenistic civilization
334	Battle at Granikos River
333	Battle at Issos River
331	Battle of Gaugamela: end of Persian power
	Alexander the Great becomes King of the Greeks and the Persians
323	Alexander the Great dies in Babylon

DATES IN ROMAN HISTORY
The Monarchy and Republic Period
ALL DATES B.C.

753	Foundation of Rome
	Kings: Romulus
	Numa Pompilius
	Tullus Hostilius
	Ancus Martius
	Tarquinius Priscus
	Servius Tullius
	Tarquinius Superbus
509	Start of the Roman Republic
494–287	Patrician-Plebeian social struggle
390	Gauls sack Rome
390–338	War with the Latins (Latium)
4th century	War with the Etruscans and other Italic tribes
343–290	Samnite Wars
287	Lex Hortensia
280–275	War with Pyrrhus
264–241	First Punic War; Sicily and Sardinia become the first Roman province
218–201	Second Punic War
216	Battle of Cannae
202	Battle of Zama; Spain becomes two Roman provinces
200–196	War in Greece
171–168	War in Greece
149–146	Third Punic War
146	Destruction of Corinth and Carthage
133	Pergamon becomes a province of Asia
	Reforms and death of Tiberius Gracchus

123	Reforms of Gaius Gracchus (killed 121 B.C.)
88	Sulla marches on Rome
87	Marius retakes Rome (dies 86 B.C.)
82	First civil war; Sulla becomes dictator (dies 78 B.C.)
73–71	Spartacus's slave revolt
70	Crassus and Pompey are consuls
63	Annexation of Syria and other areas as Roman provinces
60	First Triumvirate: alliance of Caesar, Pompey, and Crassus
58–51	Caesar in Gaul; Gallic Wars
53	Death of Crassus
49–46	Second civil war; Caesar becomes dictator
44	Death of Caesar
43	Second Triumvirate: Octavian, Mark Antony, and Lepidus
42	Death of Brutus and Cassius at Philippi
31	Battle of Actium: Octavian defeats forces of Antony and Cleopatra and becomes sole ruler of the Republic

THE ROMAN EMPIRE

Emperors

Julio-Claudian Dynasty

27 B.C.–A.D. 14	*Augustus* (new name of Octavian)

ALL DATES THAT FOLLOW ARE A.D.

14–37	*Tiberius*
37–41	*Caligula*
41–54	*Claudius*
43	Invasion of Britain
54–68	*Nero*
64	Great fire of Rome
69	Civil war

Flavian Dynasty

69–79	*Vespasian*
79–81	*Titus*
79	Eruption of Vesuvius: Pompeii and Herculaneum destroyed
81–96	*Domitian*

The "Five Good Emperors"

96–98	*Nerva*
98–117	*Trajan*
117–138	*Hadrian*
138–161	*Antoninus Pius*
161–180	*Marcus Aurelius*
	End of the Pax Romana
180–192	*Commodus*
193	Civil war

Severan Dynasty

193–211	*Septimius Severus*

211–217	*Caracalla* and *Geta*
217–218	*Macrinus*
218–222	*Elagabalus*
222–235	*Severus Alexander*
235–284	Civil war; many emperors ruled at the same time
284–305	*Diocletian* and *Maximian*
	Empire split into East and West
	Formation of the tetrarchy
301	Edict of prices
303–311	Great Persecution of Christians
306–337	*Constantine the Great:* first Christian emperor
311	Edict of Sophia: tolerance of all religions
312	Battle at the Milvian Bridge
313	Edict of Milan: in favor of Christianity
325	Council of Nicaea
330	Foundation of Constantinople
337	Constantine the Great baptized a Christian
360–363	*Julian the Apostate;* restoration of paganism
364–375	*Valentinian I* rules the West
364–378	*Valens* rules the East
378	Battle of Adrianople; Valens killed by Visigoths
379–395	*Theodosius I;* last emperor of a united empire
395	Christianity becomes the official state religion
	Permanent split of the empire into East and West
452	Attila the Hun invades Italy and is halted by Pope Leo I
475–476	*Romulus Augustulus:* last Roman emperor in the West
476	End of the Western Roman Empire
	Odovacer deposes Romulus Augustulus and is proclaimed King of Italy

THE GREEK ALPHABET

Greek is one of the languages that belongs to the Indo-European language family that includes German, English, and Italian. The alphabet, from which our own alphabet is derived through Greek and Latin, was first developed by the Phoenicians, a sea-faring people who lived on the coast of present-day Lebanon between 1200 and 800 B.C. The Phoenician alphabet consisted of 22 consonants. About 750 B.C. the Greeks took over the Phoenician alphabet and modified it to suit their language. Because the Phoenician alphabet did not have separate characters for the vowels, the Greeks adapted and systematized vowels signs. The Greek alphabet has 24 letters. While many of them look familiar, the letters are written in a different way than our own letters, which were derived from the Latin alphabet.

Letter lower case	upper case	Name	Latin equivalent
α	A	alpha	a (as in father)
β	B	beta	b
γ	Γ	gamma	g
δ	Δ	delta	d
ε	E	epsilon	e
ζ	Z	zeta	z
η	H	eta	e (as in send)
θ	Θ	theta	th
ι	I	iota	i (as in mint)
κ	K	kappa	k
λ	Λ	lambda	l
μ	M	mu	m
ν	N	nu	n
ξ	Ξ	xi	x (as in example)
o	O	omicron	o (as in lot)
π	Π	pi	p
ρ	P	rho	r
σ, ς	Σ	sigma	s
τ	T	tau	t
υ	Y	upsilon	u
φ	Φ	phi	ph
χ	X	chi	ch
ψ	Ψ	psi	ps
ω	Ω	omega	o (as in photo)

THE LATIN ALPHABET AND NUMERALS

Like Greek, Latin belongs to the Indo-European language family. The Latin alphabet was adopted from the Greek alphabet by way of the Etruscans. Our own alphabet is directly derived from the Latin alphabet. The Latin alphabet consisted of 23 letters. The letters J, U, and W were added later to our alphabet. In Latin, the letters I and V were used both as vowels and consonants and were used to write and pronounce the letters J, U, and W. The Romans used only capital letters to write their language. Lower-case letters did not appear until the Middle Ages. The Latin alphabet is:

A B C D E F G H I K L M N O P Q R S T V X Y Z

The Romans wrote numbers by using seven signs of the alphabet:

I = 1
V = 5
X = 10
L = 50
C = 100
D = 500
M = 1000

The numbers are written next to each other in descending order and are added up.
    For example: II = 2; VI = 6; LXVIII = 68.
However, if a smaller number is written in front of a larger number, the smaller number is subtracted from the larger number.
    For example: IX = 9; IV = 4; XC = 90.

The year 1995 is written MCMXCV.

Translate the following Roman numerals into Arabic numerals (the numerals we use today).

1. LXXXVIII _____   6. XVIII   _____

2. MMIX   _____   7. XLIV   _____

3. DCCII   _____   8. CCCLXXIII _____

4. DCLXI   _____   9. CDLVI   _____

5. CMXXX   _____   10. LXXXIX   _____

LATIN PHRASES AND QUOTATIONS USED IN THE ENGLISH LANGUAGE

Phrases	Translation
alter ego	one's second self
a posteriori	inductive reasoning; from effect to cause
a priori	deductive reasoning; from cause to effect
bone fide	good faith
carpe diem	seize the day; enjoy the moment
cogito, ergo sum	I think, therefore I am
de facto	existing by fact, not by right
et alia (et al.)	and other things
et cetera (etc.)	and the rest
exampli gratia (e.g.)	for example
ex gratia	performed as an act of grace
ibidem (ibid.)	the same text
idem	the same
id est (i.e.)	that is
in excelsis	in the highest
in principio	in the beginning
in situ	in the original place
inter alia	among other things
ipso facto	by the fact itself
nota bene	note well
persona (non)grata	an (un)acceptable person
quid pro quo	this for that
sine qua non	fundamental cause; necessary precondition
verbatim	word for word; exactly as quoted

Quotations	Translation
ad praesens ova cras pullis sunt meliora	eggs today are better than chickens tomorrow
ave, Caesar, morituri te salutant	Hail Caesar, those of us who are about to die salute you
veni, vidi, vici (Julius Caesar)	I came, I saw, I conquered
aut disce aut discede (Oxford)	either learn or leave
dum vivimus, viviamus	while we live, let us live
felix qui nihil debet	happy is he who owes nothing
nam et ipsa scientia potestas est (Bacon)	for knowledge is itself power
non semper ea sunt quae videntur (Phaedrus)	things are never what they seem
nosce te ipsum	know thyself
respice, adspice, prospice	look to the past, look to the present, look to the future
temporis ars medicina fere est (Ovid)	time is the best means of healing

X

KNOSSOS

This fresco depicts the sport of bull-leaping, which was popular with the people of Crete.

Legend tells of a King Minos who lived on the island of Crete in the Aegean Sea. In his palace at Knossos he had a labyrinth (maze) where a mythical beast, called the Minotaur, lived. This beast had the head of a bull and the body of a human. Annually, the king of Athens had to send seven young men and seven young maidens to King Minos as food for the Minotaur. One year, Theseus, son of the king of Athens, accompanied the young victims to Crete. After arriving at Knossos, Theseus and his companions were helped by Ariadne, King Minos's daughter, who gave him a dagger to kill the Minotaur and some thread to find his way out of the labyrinth. And so Theseus killed the beast, found his way safely out of the labyrinth, and freed Athens from the annual obligation of sending fourteen youths to Crete.

In A.D. 1900 a famous British archaeologist named Arthur Evans discovered a large palace at Knossos in north-central Crete. This palace belonged to a civilization that Evans called the Minoan civilization, named after the legendary King Minos of the labyrinth. This civilization flourished on Crete between 2000 and 1450 B.C. (See map on page 87.)

The Minoan civilization consisted of a number of palaces, the largest of which is located at Knossos. The palace had several purposes. It served as the residence of the king, who was the supreme ruler, along with his family and attendants. It was also a place where attendants and higher officials carried out the daily business of the palace and the area it controlled. Finally, food and trade items were stored there and redistributed to the common people of the countryside.

The Minoan people lived in towns and villages. Some cultivated primarily olives and grapes. Others were craftsmen and artisans. They manufactured luxury items, such as finely-painted pottery, elaborately-carved stone vessels, and jewelry. These items were traded as far away as Egypt and the Near East. Trade was an important part of Minoan life. This civilization was prosperous and technologically advanced. The palaces had an advanced drainage system complete with baths. Frescoes, or wall paintings, decorated the walls of the palaces with scenes of animals, games, and religious festivals. This indicates that the Minoans were a peaceful and fun-loving people. The Minoans loved games, such as boxing and bull-leaping. Bull-leaping involved jumping onto a bull by grabbing its horns, doing a somersault, and landing back on the ground.

About 1450 B.C. the Minoan civilization came to an end. The palaces and towns were destroyed. Archaeologists can only guess as to the cause of this destruction. About fifty years before, a volcano on the nearby island of Thera had erupted violently. It brought large amounts of ash and tidal waves to Crete. As a result, it is believed that the Aegean trading system, as well as Minoan food production, was disrupted. Today, only the ancient ruins of this once wealthy and advanced civilization remain.

Name _____ Date _____

POINTS TO PONDER

1. What would you see and experience if you were to visit the palace of Knossos during its finest period?

_____

_____

_____

_____

2. What kind of evidence, or lack of evidence, indicates that the Minoans can be considered a peaceful and fun-loving people?

_____

_____

_____

_____

3. What is believed to be the cause of the end of the Minoan civilization? Why?

_____

_____

_____

_____

4. What characterizes the Minoan civilization? Why do you think we know much about the Minoan way of life but nothing of Minoan history?

_____

_____

_____

Name _____ Date _____

CHALLENGES

1. Who discovered the Minoan civilization and when?

_____

2. After which legendary figure was the Minoan civilization named?

_____

3. What was the Minotaur?

_____

_____

4. Who was Theseus, and what did he do?

_____

_____

5. Where was the Minoan civilization located?

_____

6. Where was the largest Minoan palace located?

_____

7. What games did the Minoans enjoy?

_____

8. With which areas did the Minoans trade their goods?

_____

9. What was the function of a Minoan palace?

_____

_____

_____

10. What artifacts did the Minoans produce?

_____

_____

3

MYCENAE

Homer, the first known Greek poet, who lived about 700 B.C., wrote of another civilization that arose after the fall of the Minoan civilization. It was called the Mycenaean civilization. In his epic, the *Iliad,* Homer described the wealthy palaces where heroic kings, such as Agamemnon of Mycenae, lived. These kings waged war against the people of Troy, a walled city located on the coast of northern Turkey, on the east side of the Aegean. According to the story, the Mycenaeans defeated the Trojans in a battle inside the city walls after hiding inside a large, wooden horse (the Trojan Horse), which the Trojans were tricked into bringing inside the city gates.

The Lion Gate at Mycenae

This civilization was named after an important palace, Mycenae, located in the Peloponnese on mainland Greece (the southern region of Greece connected to the rest of the country by the Isthmus of Corinth). (See map on page 87.) It was discovered by a famous German archaeologist, Heinrich Schliemann, in A.D. 1876. The Mycenaeans were Greeks who came to the Greek mainland about 2000 B.C. By about 1500 B.C., there emerged a civilization as prosperous and wealthy as that of Minoan Crete.

The archaeological remains in the Peloponnese consist of large palaces that served the same purposes as those found on Crete. Unlike the Minoans, however, the Mycenaeans were a warlike people. The palaces were surrounded by well-built walls for defense. The frescoes on the walls show many scenes of hunting and warfare. Bronze weapons and body armor and helmets made of ivory tusks were also found among the artifacts. For survival in case of siege, the Mycenaeans built underground tunnels leading to a water well outside the palace gates. Like the Minoans, the Mycenaeans cultivated olives and grapes and traded jars of oil and wine, as well as painted pottery, throughout the Mediterranean region.

Mycenaeans buried their dead in monumental family tombs. The burial chamber of the tomb was dug into a hillside and was approached by a long tunnel-like entrance (called a *dromos*). The dead were buried with their belongings (painted pottery, gold jewelry and cups, and weapons) on the floor or in a pit of the chamber.

The Mycenaeans had a written language, which was written on rectangular clay tablets. The script is called "Linear B" because its characters consisted of lines. The tablets contain lists of food and other products made, stored, and distributed by the palace officials. They contain no historical information that can tell us of any wars or the reason for the end of this civilization. Disaster struck the palaces between about 1200 and 1100 B.C. They were destroyed by fire, and the people abandoned their homes. Many causes could have contributed to the fall of this civilization: drought, civil war, or outside invaders from the north called the Dorians. There is no evidence, however, to tell us exactly what happened.

Name _____ Date _____

POINTS TO PONDER

1. What evidence exists to indicate that the Mycenaeans were a warlike people?

_____

_____

_____

_____

2. What are the differences between the Minoan and Mycenaean civilizations?

_____

_____

_____

_____

3. What similarities do you find between the Minoan and Mycenaean civilizations?

_____

_____

_____

_____

Name _____ Date _____

CHALLENGES

1. Who were the Mycenaeans?

_____

_____

2. How did the Mycenaeans capture Troy?

_____

_____

3. Who wrote the epic of the *Iliad*?

_____

4. Who discovered the Mycenaean civilization?

_____

5. Where was the Mycenaean civilization located?

_____

_____

6. What written language did the Mycenaeans have?

_____

7. What may have caused the end of the Mycenaean civilization?

_____

_____

8. What kind of food products did the Mycenaeans cultivate?

_____

9. What type of artifacts did the Mycenaeans produce?

_____

10. What did the Mycenaeans build to survive a siege?

_____

11. Describe a Mycenaean tomb.

_____

_____

THE RISE OF HELLENIC CIVILIZATION

During the four centuries B.C. following the Mycenaean civilization, Greece fell into a period of decline. The prosperity and wealth of the Mycenaean period had gone. The flourishing arts, monumental architecture, and knowledge of writing disappeared. Trade declined, and the Mycenaean palaces were abandoned. The period is known as the "Dark Ages," and it lasted from about 1200 to 750 B.C.

Homer, who wrote about the heroic deeds of Mycenaean kings in the *Iliad,* also described the events within the social and political background of this dark period. Agriculture had returned to a simple level of subsistence. Every man owned and cultivated his own small plot of land for individual survival. The king was no longer the supreme and authoritative ruler, but was advised in regard to what action should be taken by a small group of nobles

Homer wrote about the period in Greek history known as the Dark Ages.

or aristocrats. The *monarchy* of the Mycenaean period, where the king was supreme, was replaced by a "rule of a few men," called an *oligarchy*. A small group of wealthy nobles had all the power.

Another significant change that occurred at the beginning of this period was the introduction of iron for making tools and weapons. Accordingly, this period is also known as the "Iron Age."

One major event that characterizes the "Dark Ages" was a migration of Greeks across the Aegean Sea. Thucidydes, a fifth century B.C. Greek historian, called this the Ionian Migrations. (See map on page 87.) Three groups of Greeks, based on dialects they spoke, moved to and settled on the western coast of Asia Minor (modern-day Turkey). The Dorians, who spoke Doric, settled in the southern part; the Ionians, who spoke Ionic, inhabited the middle part; and the Aeolians, who spoke Aeolic, went to the northern part of the area. The Greeks living in this coastal area were later to be the cause of conflict between the Greeks and the Persians.

By the middle of the eighth century B.C., Greece had recovered from its darkest period in history, and a new civilization emerged. This was called the Hellenic (or Greek) civilization. Trade once again began to flourish. The alphabet was introduced into Greece from Phoenicia, a seafaring state located in today's Lebanon. Because the alphabet contained no vowels, vowels were added to adapt to the Greek language. Most importantly, a new political institution emerged, which typified the rest of Greek political history—the *city-state* or *polis.* Because Greece is a very mountainous region, small independent political units developed rather than a large political union. Another factor in the development of city-states was the Greeks' love for freedom and independence. Each city-state was autonomous with its own laws and constitution, leaders and army, system of taxation, and sometimes its own coinage system. The largest and most important of Greek city-states

7

were Athens in Attica, Sparta in the Peloponnese, and Thebes in Boeotia.

Until about 650 B.C., most city-states were ruled by the aristocrats. They had an oligarchic form of government. The political power was in the hands of a few wealthy families who owned the best land and abused the majority of the city-state's citizens who were poor farmers. Sometimes these farmers got into debt and were forced to work for the aristocrats to pay off their debts. Some even became slaves.

Starting about 750 B.C., due to poverty and insufficient farming land, these poor farmers began to leave their homelands and seek new opportunities elsewhere. Other reasons for emigration, even though less important, were trade, personal adventure, and political refuge. A phase of "Greek colonization" was launched. (See inset map on page 87.) Colonies were set up along the coasts of southern Italy and Sicily (known as Magna Graecia or Greater Greece), France, Spain, and along the coast of the northern Aegean and Black Seas. Some important colonies include Syracuse (Sicily), Phaestum and Cumae (Italy), Massalia (modern Marseille, France), and Byzantium on the Black Sea (modern Istanbul). The Greek city-states that took part in this colonization process were mostly Athens, Corinth in the Peloponnese, Eretria and Chalkis on the island of Euboea, and the Greek-Asiatic cities of Miletus and Phocaea. The Greek colonies became city-states of their own and were politically and economically independent. The only ties that remained with their mother city-states were cultural and religious. By 600 B.C. the Greeks had spread their people and ideas throughout the regions of the Mediterranean and Black Seas. This Greek influence was later to have a profound effect on Roman culture.

One of the results of Greek colonization was the emergence of a new social class of people, the middle class or merchants, who had become wealthy through industry and trade. This new middle class also wanted a share in the political power of the city-states. Consequently, at home in Greece, the discontent of the poor was solved in another way. Tyrants, men from the new middle class, came to power in many city-states between 650 and 500 B.C. with the support of the people. This type of government is called a *tyranny*. A Greek tyrant, however, unlike today's tyrant, was not a brutal ruler, but a ruler who had not taken power according to the constitution. In fact, most Greek tyrants were good rulers and brought many benefits, such as power and wealth, to the city-states. Coinage was introduced, trade and colonization were encouraged, and athletic, musical, and dramatic contests were established. One notable tyrant was Peisistratus of Athens (560–529 B.C.), who embellished the city with monuments, stimulated trade and industry, and helped the poor farmers. He increased the prestige of Athens.

A very important change that took place during this time, and one which may also have helped the rise in power of tyrants, was the development of an infantry army. A new type of heavily-armed soldier (*hoplite*), placed within a tight formation, called a *phalanx*, fought many successful battles for the next three centuries.

The rule of tyrannies did not last very long, however, because some of the tyrants in power became too authoritarian. Instead, the governments of the city-states became once again oligarchies or changed to a new form of rule, *democracy*. Democracy, or "rule by the people," was first developed in Athens. Sparta, on the other hand, retained a form of oligarchic rule. The other Greek city-states followed the lead of either Athens or Sparta.

Name _____ Date _____

POINTS TO PONDER

1. Why did the Hellenic civilization develop the political institution of the city-state or polis? Describe the function of a city-state. What effect do you think this kind of political setup will have on the political history of Greece?

_____

_____

_____

_____

2. Explain the main reason for Greek colonization. What other factors were involved in Greek settlement abroad?

_____

_____

_____

_____

3. Describe the term *tyrant* as it was originally used in Greek history. Compare it to a tyrant in today's society.

_____

_____

_____

_____

4. Why is the period following the Mycenaean period called the "Dark Age" or the "Iron Age"?

_____

_____

_____

_____

Name _____ Date _____

CHALLENGES

1. What are the three developments that led to the recovery of Greek civilization by 750 B.C.?

_____

_____

2. What significant change took place in the Dark Age period?

_____

3. What major event characterizes the Dark Age period?

_____

4. Who were the three groups of Greeks that took part in the Ionian Migration?

_____

5. What were the three largest and most-important city-states in Greece?

_____

6. Where did the Greeks colonize?

_____

_____

_____

7. Which Greek cities were involved in setting up colonies?

_____

8. What new social class emerged as a result of Greek colonization?

_____

9. Who was Peisistratus?

_____

10. Name three Greek colonies.

_____

11. What is a monarchy?

_____

12. What is an oligarchy?

_____

LYCURGUS AND SPARTA

According to the Spartans, about 700 B.C. a semi-legendary figure named Lycurgus established a number of social and political institutions that made Sparta a great power of Greece.

He started an educational system that produced men of military strength and loyal soldiers. It all began at birth. If a newly-born baby was weak or sickly, it was abandoned and left to die on a mountain slope. At the age of seven, a boy came under the control of the city and remained so until his death. He was to live together with the other boys in a camp, and the training process started. The boys learned to read and write and were taught music and poetry. Most importantly, however, they were taught discipline, courage, and virtue. Each boy exercised a lot and competed in violent games and fights. They were forced to steal, but if caught, the boys were punished for being careless and unskillful. Their

Heavily-armed hoplites became the backbone of Greek armies.

training continued into manhood. The girls were also brought up in a strict manner. They had to exercise their bodies to make them grow strong in order to be able to deal easily with childbirth.

Sparta did not adopt a coinage system like other Greek cities because wealth was not desirable and was regarded without envy and prestige. Trade was forbidden both within and outside the city. Every citizen had an equal share of land to live on. They were also forbidden to travel, except on army expeditions during times of war, in order that they might not be exposed to foreign behaviors and ideas. The Spartans were very patriotic Greeks and fought for their state until their death. They had adopted a system of living where there was little individual freedom and where order and discipline ruled.

Lycurgus also set up a type of government at Sparta that was a form of oligarchy. A few wealthy aristocrats held the power, but the city's constitution retained its kings of the previous age. No individual was able to become too powerful. The government consisted of two *kings* who were the generals of the army. The executive power lay in the hands of five magistrates, called *ephors.* The ephors were the judges of the city and dealt with internal and foreign affairs. They obtained advice from the *council of elders,* which consisted of 28 ex-magistrates. A second council of the Spartan people (*Spartiates*), called the *assembly,* also existed. This council had the right to reject or approve any proposals put before them.

Sparta controlled about two-fifths of the Peloponnese. During the eighth century B.C., Sparta conquered Laconia and Messenia and their inhabitants. (See map on page 87.) In the Spartan social structure, these inhabitants were divided into two groups: the *helots,* who were slaves who worked the land to supply food for the Spartiates, and the *perioiki,* who were freedmen but were socially inferior. Both groups would also have to join the Spartan army in times of war.

Name _____ Date _____

POINTS TO PONDER

1. Describe the constitution of Sparta. Do you think that equality existed in the Spartan social and political system? Why or why not?

_____

_____

_____

_____

_____

2. Describe the lifestyle of a Spartan. Would you have liked to have been a Spartan? Why or why not?

_____

_____

_____

_____

_____

3. Why were the Spartans not allowed to trade or travel? How do you think this may have affected Sparta culturally and economically?

_____

_____

_____

_____

_____

Name _____ Date _____

CHALLENGES

1. Who was Lycurgus?

_____

2. What was the purpose of the educational system in Sparta?

_____

3. Who set up the social and political system of Sparta?

_____

4. Who were the helots?

_____

_____

5. Who were the perioiki?

_____

_____

6. Who were the Spartiates?

_____

7. Who were the real rulers of Sparta?

_____

8. What was the function of the council of elders?

_____

_____

9. What was the function of the two kings?

_____

_____

10. What was the function of the assembly?

_____

_____

ATHENS AND DEMOCRACY

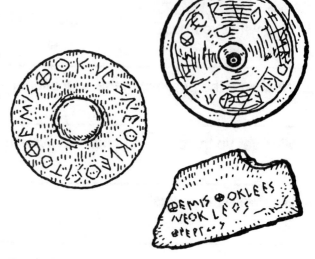

The oligarchy of Sparta was radically different from the type of government practiced by the Athenians, who set up a *democracy*. The constitution was not in the hands of the few; rather, it was controlled by the many—the *demos* or people. Four men were responsible for the development of democracy in Athens. Solon, in 594 B.C., was the first. He made social and political reforms to lessen the conflict between the rich and poor in the city. In order to free all citizens from debt and enslavement, he cancelled all debts and abolished slavery. Politically, he re-

Examples of ostraka (potshards) cast against Themistocles

duced the power of the wealthy aristocrats by giving more power to the people.

The government already consisted of two leaders called *archons* who held the executive power. These men were advised by an aristocratic council of elders called the Council of the Areopagus (the Areopagus was a hill in Athens where its meetings were held). To these Solon now added three new political bodies that gave more power to the average citizen: a People's Court where all disputes, public or private, were settled by the people; the People's Assembly (to which all Athenian citizens belonged) that decided on the matters of the state; and a Council of 400 (which consisted of 100 citizens from each of the four tribes that made up the Athenian citizenry) that prepared business for the Assembly to consider. Solon's reforms, however, pleased neither the populace, because not enough power was given, nor the aristocrats, because their power was decreased. Unrest followed.

Peisistratus then became tyrant in 560 B.C. Among his benefits to the city, he continued the process of democratization by redistributing the land (previously owned by the rich nobles) to farmers and making loans to poor farmers to start anew.

In 508 B.C. a third influential figure, Cleisthenes, came to power in Athens. He did much to develop Athenian democracy. Cleisthenes divided the citizens into ten new tribes (from the four old tribes) and mixed them up so that no one tribe was dominated by the rich as had been the case before. He increased the Council of 400 to the Council of 500, which now consisted of 50 citizens from each tribe. He also introduced the practice of *ostracism*. Every year the Athenians could banish from the city any man they deemed threatening. This was done by writing his name on a potshard or *ostraka*. The man with the most votes was then exiled for ten years.

It was in the time of Pericles (461–429 B.C.), one of Athens' best statesmen, that democracy was completely attained. He made all offices in the government payable, and all officers were elected by lot rather than by vote, so that even the poorest citizens now could participate in the government.

Athenian democracy has influenced many democratic goverments in world history, including the American governmental system.

14

Name _____ Date _____

POINTS TO PONDER

1. What was the purpose of setting up a democracy in Athens, and how did it develop?

_____

_____

_____

_____

_____

2. Of the four Athenian leaders, who do you think made the most effective changes in giving the people power in the government? Why?

_____

_____

_____

_____

_____

3. What differences and similarities do you detect between the Spartan and Athenian governments?

_____

_____

_____

_____

_____

Name _____ Date _____

CHALLENGES

1. Define democracy.

_____

2. In which city was democracy first developed?

_____

3. Which Athenian leaders were responsible for the development of democracy?

_____

_____

4. Why was the aristocratic council of elders called the Council of the Areopagus?

_____

_____

5. What is ostracism?

_____

_____

6. Who were the real leaders of Athens?

_____

7. Which government today was influenced by the Athenian democracy?

_____

8. Who divided up the citizens of Athens into ten new tribes from the four old ones?

_____

9. Which Athenian leader started off the process of democracy?

_____

10. Why were Solon's reforms not completely successful in appeasing the aristocracy and the people?

_____

_____

_____

THE WARS WITH PERSIA

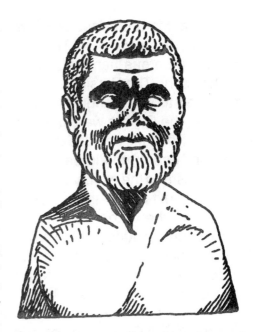

About 1000 B.C. an Indo-European people called the Persians occupied the area east of the Tigris River in western Asia. They became a powerful nation during the sixth century B.C. under King Cyrus the Great (559–529 B.C.). Cyrus not only made Persia a strong empire in western Asia, but also expanded Persian rule to include most of western Asia up to the Indus River. The Greek cities on the western coast of Asia Minor were also conquered by Cyrus and became subjects of the Persians. His sons, Cambyses (529–522 B.C.) and Darius (522–486 B.C.), who succeeded him on the throne of Persia, expanded the empire to include Egypt and northern Greece. By about 500 B.C. Persia extended from the Mediterranean Sea in the west to the edge of India in the east and from the Black Sea in the north to the Persian Gulf in the south. (See map on page 88.) It was organized

Themistocles led the Athenian fleet in its victory over the Persians at the Battle of Salamis.

into 20 provinces called *satrapies,* each ruled by a *satrap* or governor. Trade and communication were made efficient (and thus aided in the ruling of the empire) by the building of the Royal Road, which ran from the first capital city, Sousa, to Sardis. Not much later, the capital was moved to Persepolis under King Xerxes (486–465 B.C.), son of Darius.

The Greeks in Asia Minor were not very happy under Persian rule and wanted freedom. Therefore, they decided to revolt against their foreign rulers in 499 B.C. Thus began the Ionian Revolt, which was the beginning of the fighting between the Greeks and Persians, known as the Persian Wars. The Persian Wars were described in detail by the first known Greek historian, Herodotus, in the fifth century B.C. The Ionian Revolt was started by Aristagoras, tyrant of the Greek city of Miletus, who spurred on the other Ionian cities to rise up against the Persians. (See map on page 87.) The Ionian Greeks, realizing they needed help from the mainland Greeks to accomplish their goal, asked both Sparta and Athens for ships and men. Only Athens and its ally Eretria in Euboea were willing to help, and they sent out 25 manned ships. The aid, however, was too little, and after a major defeat, the Greek allies were forced to withdraw. The uprising ended when Miletus was sacked by the Persians in 494 B.C. The revolt had failed, and the Ionian Greeks were back under Persian control. However, as Herodotus said, this incident was the beginning of trouble for both the Greeks and the Persians.

Darius, King of the Persians at this time, partially intending to punish the Athenians for their aid to the Asiatic Greeks and partially to expand Persian rule into Europe, decided to invade mainland Greece. This first expedition occurred in 492 B.C., but was a disaster. The Persian fleet was wrecked in a major storm off the Aegean coast in northern Greece. In 490 B.C. Darius and his Persian troops tried again and sailed instead across the Aegean Sea. On their way to take Athens, they first besieged and captured Eretria in Euboea and from there sailed across to the east coast of Attica to the bay of Marathon. The Greeks, with the exception of the Spartans who were busy with a religious festival, went out to meet the

Persians at Marathon instead of waiting for them to come to Athens. The first land battle of the Persian Wars followed. This was the Battle of Marathon. Even though the Persians were far more numerous than the Greeks in manpower, Athenian battle tactics allowed for a major Greek victory. The Persian ships, which were not captured by the Greeks after the battle, proceeded to sail around Attica in order to take Athens while the city was unprotected. However, the Greeks were quicker and returned to defend Athens by that evening. At this point, the Persians decided to withdraw and return to Asia. Darius's second expedition had failed, and Greek morale was high. The victory at Marathon had shown the Greeks that they could withstand the mighty Persians. The Persians, however, were to return ten years later under the next ruler, King Xerxes.

After the victory at Marathon, Athens began to build up a strong navy in case of another Persian attack. This was accomplished by the great politician of Athens at that time, Themistocles. Two hundred new warships called *triremes* were built. A trireme was a ship of about 120 feet long and 12 feet wide that was driven by three sets of oars. Each trireme had a crew of 170 rowers, a boatswain, a helmsman, 20 marines, and a few officers.

In 480 B.C. the Persians returned to fight another war. Xerxes was determined to take revenge on the Greeks and decided to invade. He crossed the Hellespont, then both his army and his fleet advanced along the Aegean coast and finally down into Greece. The first battles between the Greeks and the Persians were fought both by land and sea. The sea battle took place at Cape Artemision, north of Euboea. At the same time, a land battle was fought at Thermopylae, a narrow pass between Thessaly and Boeotia that the Persians had to cross to reach Athens. At this battle three hundred Spartans led by King Leonidas met their deaths at the hands of the Persians. The main Greek forces had not arrived in time for the battle. The Spartan soldiers put up a noble resistance. None tried to retreat but fought till the last man fell, showing the bravery and courage of the Spartan soldier. This battle is considered the most "glorious" defeat in Greek history. After the Persian victory at Thermopylae, the Persian forces were now in control of central Greece and were on the way to occupying and destroying Athens.

Meanwhile in Athens, Themistocles persuaded most of the Athenians to evacuate the city and assemble the Athenian fleet at Salamis, an island off the coast of Athens. The Delphic oracle (an oracle located in the sanctuary of Apollo in Delphi where the Greeks could get advice on any matter they wished, with the answers given in the form of riddles) had told Themistocles that Athens would be saved by "wooden walls," which he took to mean a wall of ships. When the Persians found the city of Athens deserted, they set fire to it and destroyed it. They soon were tricked by Themistocles into fighting the Athenians in the bay of Salamis. The Battle of Salamis was chaotic and bloody. "The sea was full of wreckage and blood. . . . never in one day did such a multitude of men die." (Herodotus, VII, 420ff.) At the end, the Athenians were victorious and Xerxes ordered his Persian troops to withdraw. He himself went back to Persia, but left behind a Persian land force in northern Greece. A year later in 479 B.C., the Greek army attacked and defeated the remaining Persian army at the Battle of Plataea, in Boeotia. The Persians were forced to withdraw back to Persia. The last action of the Persian Wars, supposedly fought on the same day as the Battle of Plataea, was a sea battle at Cape Mycale in Ionia, where the remainder of the Persian fleet was destroyed. The war was finished. The Greeks were victorious in driving the Persians out of Greece. They had liberated their land from the barbarians.

Name _____ Date _____

POINTS TO PONDER

1. Why were the Greeks able to defeat the Persians despite being outnumbered?

_____

_____

_____

_____

_____

2. Describe how the Ionians were responsible for the start of the Persian Wars.

_____

_____

_____

_____

_____

3. Why was Thermopylae considered a most "glorious" defeat?

_____

_____

_____

_____

_____

Name _____ Date _____

CHALLENGES

1. Who made the Persians a powerful nation in western Asia?

_____

2. Which kings were responsible for the expansion of the Persian Empire?

_____

3. Describe the extent of the Persian Empire about 500 B.C.

_____

_____

4. What is a satrap?

_____

5. How were the Persians able to control such a large area?

_____

6. What was the capital of the Persians?

_____

7. What event started the Persian Wars?

_____

8. Who wrote about the history of the Persian Wars?

_____

9. Which battle is considered the most glorious defeat in Greek history?

_____

10. What is a trireme?

_____

11. Who was the king of Persia during the first part of the Persian Wars?

_____

12. Who was the king of Persia during the last part of the Persian Wars?

_____

13. Why did the Persians invade Greece?

_____

_____

THE PELOPONNESIAN WAR AND ITS AFTERMATH

The remainder of the fifth century B.C. was dominated by another great war. It was a war between the two biggest powers of Greece: Athens and Sparta. The growth and collapse of Athenian seapower was the focus of this period in Greek history, which was reported by the second great Greek historian of the fifth century B.C., Thucydides.

The Persian Wars gave the Greeks pride and a new self-confidence that led to great achievements in the following years. After the war, Athens became the leading Greek city-state. It began when she set up a league of Asiatic Greek city-states called the Delian League. It protected Ionia and the rest of Greece against any further attack from the Persians. Athens acquired the league's leadership and the cities within the league were obliged to contribute either money or ships. The purpose of the league was to take revenge on the Persians for the sufferings they had caused and liberate all Asiatic and

Under Pericles' leadership Athens became the cultural and political center of Greece in the fifth century B.C.

other Greek cities still under Persian control. By 468 B.C. all Greek cities along the Aegean coast were liberated and the Persian fleet was demolished. However, when the mission of the league was accomplished, Athens did not renounce the Delian League. Instead she began forcing the liberated Greek cities to stay in the league under her control. In addition, Athens forced other cities to join the league. Athens thus became the leader of an Athenian sea empire and the greatest power in Greece.

It was the Athenian leader Pericles (461–429 B.C.) who was responsible for Athens' growth in power. He also made Athens the cultural center of Greece. A building program was begun that included the Parthenon on the Acropolis, a temple dedicated to the city's patron goddess Athena. He also connected Athens and its port, Piraeus, by long walls to protect the city against attacks. With his ambitious political policy, he was responsible for bringing Athens into a war against Sparta.

By 500 B.C. Sparta had established her own league, called the Peloponnesian League, which consisted mostly of cities in the Peloponnese. According to Thucydides, it was Sparta's fear of Athenian power that made war between the two city-states inevitable. This war, called the Peloponnesian War, broke out in 431 B.C. and continued for 27 years with a short break between 421 and 415 B.C. The whole of Greece was involved in the war. Athens and her allies (the Delian League) fought on one side of the war and Sparta and her allies (the Peloponnesian League) on the other. (See map on page 87.)

During the first part of the war (431–421 B.C.), Sparta continually ravaged the countryside of Attica, but it had little effect on Athens. No decisive victory on either side was achieved during those ten years. However, plagues hit Athens twice during this time and killed a third of her population. One of the victims was Pericles. This was a critical turning point in Athens' destiny. Having lost one of her greatest generals and most-experienced politicians, Athens gradually lost control over her sea empire.

A truce was concluded between the two powers in 421 B.C., but war broke out again in 415 B.C. and lasted until 404 B.C. It began when both Athens and Sparta and their allies became involved in a war between some of the Greek city-states in Sicily. Athens sent out a big expedition and after two years of fighting, met with the greatest defeat in Athenian history. She not only lost many men, but also her whole fleet. This incident made Athens' final defeat unavoidable. During the last years of the war, despite some successes in battle, Athens' power diminished. Many of her allies revolted. Her treasury was empty of funds needed for the war. An oligarchic revolution in 411 B.C. brought about internal problems. Finally, Sparta received monetary help from the Persians to insure victory. In 405 B.C. a decisive battle near the Hellespont, the Battle of Aegospotami, insured victory for the Spartans. The Athenians surrendered a year later. They had lost the war and their once-mighty sea empire. Peace was declared, and Sparta set up an oligarchic rule in Athens called the Rule of the Thirty or Thirty Tyrants. This rule did not last very long, and democracy was restored in Athens in 403 B.C. After the defeat of Athens in the Peloponnesian War, Sparta now became the leading power in Greece, taking over the empire once ruled by Athens.

At this point in Greek history, the Greek historian Xenophon takes over the account of Greece during the fourth century B.C. The fourth century is characterized by the rivalry between various Greek city-states, most prominently Sparta, Athens, and Thebes in various alliances. This conflict between the city-states eventually weakened the Greeks and led to the takeover of Greece by the King of Macedon, Philip II, in 338 B.C.

Between 395 and 386 B.C., Athens, in alliance with Thebes and other city-states with the support of Persia, was involved in a war to put down Sparta's growing power. Peace was subsequently imposed temporarily in 386 B.C. by the King of Persia. This was called the King's Peace. The terms included the abandonment of all Asiatic Greek city-states back to Persia. The peace did allow Sparta to continue its dominant power in Greece; however, Sparta's arrogance led to more fighting, and finally, her power was destroyed at the Battle of Leuctra in 371 B.C. by the Thebans.

Thebes was under the rule of a very skilled general named Epaminondas, who made his city the center of power in Greece for a short time. However, in 362 B.C. the allied forces of Sparta and Athens fought against Thebes at the Battle of Mantinea, and even though the Thebans won the battle, Epaminondas was killed. Since there was no one to replace his excellent leadership, Thebes' brief period of dominance came to an end. Fighting between various city-states continued until 338 B.C., and no one city-state was stronger than another.

In the meantime another state in the north, Macedonia, was rising to power under its king, Philip II. In 359 B.C. he united the Macedonian state and built up a loyal and professional army, which brought him great successes in battle. While the Greek city-states were quarreling among themselves, Philip extended his influence over the whole of Greece. Except for one man, the orator Demosthenes, no one in Athens foresaw Philip's actions of conquest. Philip eventually conquered the Greeks in 338 B.C. at the Battle of Chaeronea. By then the Greeks were too weak and disorganized to stand up to him.

Name _____ Date _____

POINTS TO PONDER

1. Why did Athens become the leading power of Greece after the Persian Wars? Why do you think Sparta did not become the leading Greek city-state?

_____

_____

_____

_____

2. What were the reasons for Athens' defeat in the Peloponnesian War?

_____

_____

_____

_____

3. What characterizes the fourth century period in Greek history? What was the result?

_____

_____

_____

_____

Name _____ Date _____

CHALLENGES

1. Which two powers were involved in the Peloponnesian War?

_____

2. Who was responsible for the growth of Athenian power?

_____

3. What was the Delian League?

_____

_____

4. What was the purpose of the Delian League?

_____

_____

5. Who wrote about the Peloponnesian War?

_____

6. Who won the Peloponnesian War?

_____

7. What was the last battle of the Peloponnesian War?

_____

8. Who was Epaminondas?

_____

_____

9. Who was Philip II?

_____

_____

10. In what battle did Philip II defeat the Greeks?

_____

ALEXANDER THE GREAT

After his conquest of Greece, Philip II of Macedon intended to conquer the Persians and their empire. He died in 336 B.C., however, before he was able to carry out his plan. His son, Alexander, later called "the Great," took over this task and was successful. His achievements are told by the contemporary historian Arrian in his *Anabasis.*

Alexander was 20 years old when he came to the throne of Macedon. He was a very ambitious man and a great general like his father. Just two years later he set out to conquer the Persian Empire, which was ruled by King Darius III. With an army of about 35,000 men, he entered Asia Minor and moved south through Syria, Palestine, and Egypt, defeating the Persians in battle at the Granikos River in 334 B.C. and the Issos River in the following year. He occupied Egypt in 332 B.C. where he spent the winter. In 331 he marched further inland to the Tigris River. At Gaugamela that same year, he had a decisive victory over Darius III in battle. Alexander was now "King of the Greeks and the Persians." Over the next three years, the king continued his march south

Alexander conquered an empire that stretched from Macedonia to Egypt to the Indus River, but he was unable to enjoy the fruits of his labors as he died at the age of 32.

and then proceeded eastward toward the Indus River, subduing the eastern part of the Persian Empire. He passed through the cities of Babylon, Sousa, Persepolis, and Ecbatana. (See map on page 88.) In 327 B.C. Alexander planned to invade India and crossed the Indus River a year later, but his army was getting tired from the long expedition and all the fighting on the way, so they revolted against him. Alexander was forced to turn back toward Macedonia in 325 B.C. On his way back in 323, while staying in Babylon, Alexander died at the young age of 32. During his campaign into Asia, he had suffered many wounds and sicknesses, and it is said that his weakness made him vulnerable to malaria. Others say that he was poisoned.

Alexander the Great was indeed a great ruler. His dream was to unify East and West, which he succeeded in doing. He ruled his empire well. He included Greeks and Persians in his administration. Most importantly, Greek culture was spread far and wide throughout the East. Many Greeks settled in Persia, and the cities were organized along Greek lines. He also founded many cities along the way, all called Alexandria. The finest city was the Alexandria located on the mouth of the Nile Delta in Egypt. It became the most important trading port in the Mediterranean. A variety of goods from as far away as India passed through this port. Hence, the Hellenistic civilization (336–30 B.C.) was created and lasted until the Romans conquered the whole area. Alexander the Great was one of the most influential and powerful figures in history and is regarded as one of the greatest conquerors in world history. He left behind a legacy that influenced Roman civilization and, subsequently, the Byzantine Empire.

Name _____ Date _____

POINTS TO PONDER

1. Trace Alexander's route of conquest. Can you think of other conquerors in history who have matched Alexander's achievements in a similar length of time?

_____

_____

_____

_____

2. Do you think Alexander deserved the title "the Great"? Why or why not?

_____

_____

_____

_____

3. Using an atlas, work out which modern countries were wholly or partly within the area of Alexander's empire.

_____

_____

_____

_____

Name _____ Date _____

CHALLENGES

1. Who was Alexander the Great?

_____

_____

2. Who was the last king of the Persian Empire?

_____

3. Where did Alexander die?

_____

4. In which battle did Alexander defeat Darius III?

_____

5. When did Alexander become King of the Greeks and the Persians?

_____

6. What was the name of the cities he founded throughout his empire?

_____

7. How far did Alexander's conquests take him?

_____

_____

8. Why did Alexander have to delay his conquests into India?

_____

_____

9. Who wrote about the life and history of Alexander the Great? What was his work called?

_____

_____

10. How did Alexander die?

_____

_____

GREEK ART AND ARCHITECTURE

The Acropolis: (1) the Parthenon; (2) the Erechtheion; (3) statue of Athena Promachos by Pheidias

Athens was considered the cultural center of ancient Greece. The city best exemplifies the typical architecture to be seen in a Greek city-state.

Towering above the city of Athens stood the *Acropolis,* the sacred hill dedicated to the city's patron-goddess, Athena. Below the Acropolis lay the *Agora,* the commercial and political center of the city. During the fifth century B.C. at the peak of Athens' political power, Pericles initiated the construction of many public buildings to replace the ones destroyed during the Persian Wars. These monuments still stand today and are admired by many tourists who visit Greece.

Among the most impressive buildings is the temple dedicated to Athena Parthenos on the Acropolis, the *Parthenon.* In the construction of this temple, perfection in both technical skill and proportion in design was achieved. The Parthenon housed the golden and ivory statue of Athena, which was created by the famous sculptor Pheidias. Other temples in the city included the *Erechtheion* on the Arcropolis, dedicated to both Athena and Erechteus (a legendary king of Athens); the *Hephaisteion* in the Agora, a temple dedicated to the god of crafts, Hephaestus; and the *Olympeion,* the temple dedicated to the almighty king of gods, Zeus. Each city-state had fine temples, but none exemplify Greek architecture better than those of Athens.

The Greek temple was the most important public building in any city. Its purpose was to house the statue of the patron-god or goddess and sometimes to keep the offerings made to the deity. Outside and in front of the temple lay the altar where the worshippers gathered and sacrifices were carried out. The temples were built of big limestone or marble blocks and stood on a low stone platform that could be reached by steps. The standard temple plan was rectangular in shape with a central windowless room, called the *naos.* In this room stood the deity's statue. The naos opened out onto a porch with columns (*pronaos*). The central part of the temple was encircled by a row of columns that formed the *colonnade* or covered walkway. The superstructure of the temple consisted of four main parts: the column, the architrave, the frieze, and the cornice (roof). Traces of color on building blocks indicate that parts of the temple were painted in bright colors such as reds, yellows, and blues.

Three different styles of decoration developed in Greek temples throughout the centuries. Temples originated in the seventh century B.C. with the Doric order. About 500 B.C. the Ionic order developed, and in the fourth century B.C., the Corinthian order was introduced. Although the three styles were created in progressive order, one style did not replace the other.

The orders are distinguished mainly by their columns. A column was made up of the shaft and the capital. In the Doric order, the capital was plain. The capital of the Ionic order had a *volute* (a decoration in the form of ram's horns) with an egg-and-dart pattern underneath. The Corinthian capital was decorated with acanthus leaves growing from the shaft. The frieze, which lay between the cornice and the architrave, was decorated with stone carvings. In the Doric order, it was divided into panels (*metopes*) separated by three vertical grooves (*triglyphs*), while in the Ionic order, the frieze was decorated with a continuous strip. Whereas the architrave was plain in the Doric order, in the Ionic order, it was divided into three equally-wide horizontal sections. The Corinthian order had only the capital as its distinguishing feature. The rest of the superstructure was taken over from the Ionic order. The roof of the temple, known as the cornice, was triangular in shape. It consisted of the pediment and the geison, which are the outer edges of the roof. The pediment was always filled with sculptures that represented stories related to the temple's deity, such as the birth of Athena on the Parthenon. The sculptures were brightly painted like the building parts of the temple itself. The three Greek architectural styles, especially the columns, have often been copied in the architecture of subsequent periods and in modern times.

The Greeks were not only great architects but also great sculptors. As already mentioned above, the temples were decorated with sculpted carvings, and a statue of the deity stood inside the building. One famous sculptor, mentioned earlier, was Pheidias, who made the statue of Athena entirely out of gold and ivory. Nothing of this statue remains, but descriptions exist in literature and from Roman copies. Most temple statues, however, were made of marble or bronze. Female and male statues of gods, heroes, and Olympic victors (mostly nude) also decorated many of the houses and public buildings or lined the streets. The statues were life-sized figures sculpted either from marble or cast in bronze. Detail was stressed and natural movement and appearance were emphasized. Many of the original statues have not survived, because they were either broken or, in the case of bronze, melted and reused. However, Roman copies have survived, and they provide valuable information about the original Greek works.

Pottery was another important form of Greek art. It was widely traded throughout the Mediterranean. It came in a variety of shapes depending on the practical purpose. Pottery was used to transport perishable goods such as wine, olive oil, grain, or perfume. It was also used in domestic activities such as cooking and eating or in religious ceremonies to carry offerings to the gods and as offerings in temples and tombs. Sometimes it was made and traded solely for its artistic merit. Pottery provides useful information for the historian, because many of the vases were painted with scenes of daily life, athletic activities, religious ceremonies, or mythological subjects. Like all forms of Greek art and architecture, Greek pottery production reached its height during the fifth century B.C. Two popular types of pottery were produced: Black Figure and Red Figure pottery. The clay used to make the pottery was fired red in color, due to its high iron content. In Black Figure, the figures were drawn in black on the red background. In Red Figure, the reverse was true. The figures, outlined in black, were left red on a black-glazed background. Writing was common on pots either to mark the potter's name, to indicate names of mythological or historical figures shown, or to describe the subject matter.

Today, Greek architecture, sculpture, and pottery are highly valued as historical evidence and as skilled works of art.

Architectural Orders and Parts of a Greek Temple

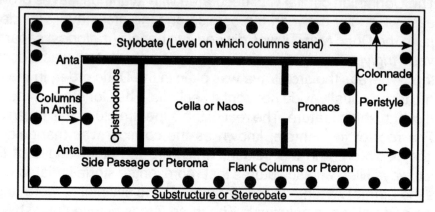

Stylobate (Level on which columns stand)

Anta

Opisthodomos

Columns in Antis

Cella or Naos

Pronaos

Colonnade or Peristyle

Anta

Side Passage or Pteroma   Flank Columns or Pteron

Substructure or Stereobate

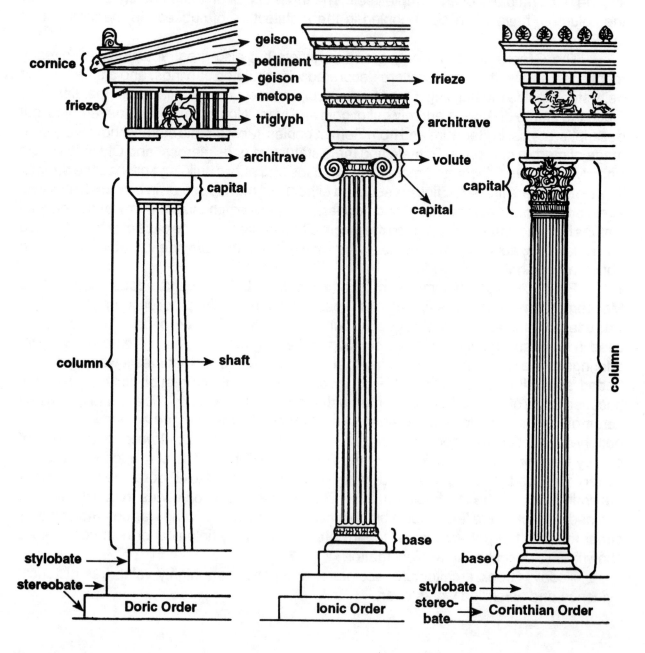

cornice {

frieze

geison
pediment
geison
metope
triglyph

architrave

capital

column {   → shaft

Doric Order

stylobate
stereobate

→ frieze

architrave

→ volute

capital

base

Ionic Order

capital

column

base

stylobate
stereo-
bate

Corinthian Order

Name _____ Date _____

POINTS TO PONDER

1. What differences do you detect between the three orders of Greek architecture?

_____

_____

_____

_____

_____

2. Was a Greek temple like a cathedral or church either in appearance or in the way it was used? Explain.

_____

_____

_____

_____

_____

3. Look at buildings in your neighborhood or nearest city and find examples of architectural features that show the influence of Greek architecture. List some of them.

_____

_____

_____

_____

_____

31

Name _____ Date _____

CHALLENGES

1. Which two main areas of cultural importance existed in Athens?

_____

2. Which temple in Athens is the most impressive?

_____

3. What is the most important public building in any Greek city-state?

_____

4. What was the purpose of the temple?

_____

_____

5. In which part of the temple did the statue of the god or goddess stand?

_____

6. Name the three orders of Greek architecture.

_____

7. Who made the golden and ivory statue of Athena Parthenos?

_____

8. What is the most distinguishable feature of each of the three architectural orders?

_____

_____

_____

9. What two popular types of pottery did the Athenians produce?

_____

10. Where were the statues of people and gods placed?

_____

_____

THEATER AND GAMES

Each year the Greeks looked forward to being entertained at several festivals held in honor of the gods. The festivals were mainly religious events. A festival consisted partially of a procession and sacrifices to the god being honored. It was also a social occasion for the Greeks to get together and enjoy the excitement of plays and athletic events.

The main social event of some of the festivals was the dramatic competition. Examples of such festivals in Athens include the festival of the City Dionysia, held in honor of Dionysus (god of wine and drama), and the Great Panathenaic Festival, held in honor of the city's patron-goddess, Athena.

Drama, an important contribution to Western civilization, was invented by the Greeks. Greek playwrights produced a large number of high-quality plays, some of which have survived in today's literature. The plays were of two kinds: tragedies and comedies. In tragedies, the subject matter dealt mostly with mythological stories,

Olympic athletes competed in eight different types of competition.

although some plays were based on historical events. The themes of the stories consisted of disasters, bloody revenge, or the suffering of the human conscience. The comedies dealt with the ridiculing of political or social issues at hand. In a public performance, only three actors played the various characters in a play. Masks were used to distinguish one character from the other, which made it easier for one actor to play several roles. Essential to all the plays was the *chorus.* The chorus was a group of performers who danced and sang at intervals throughout the play, commenting on the events of the play.

Fifth century Greece produced some of history's finest playwrights. They include Aeschylus, Sophocles, and Euripides (the tragedians) and Aristophanes (the comic poet).

One famous Greek tragedy was *Oedipus the King* by Sophocles. It tells of Oedipus, the son of a king, who was told by the Delphic oracle that he would kill his father and marry his mother. The prophesy was fulfilled, and at the end he gouged out his eyes with his mother's (wife's) broach. The play ends with his life in ruins.

One of Aeschylus's surviving plays, *The Persians,* dealt with the historical battle of Salamis in 480 B.C. The battle was described so vividly that he must have been an eyewitness of the event, if not a participant, as well.

Aristophanes is famous for his parodies of his rival playwrights, philosophers, and statesmen, as well as for making a mockery of the Athenian democracy. The plots of his plays were outlandish, sometimes involving talking animals. He used vulgar language and made obscene jokes.

The building in which the plays were held was the theater. The Greek theater was a semi-circular structure, usually built on the slope of a hill. The main feature of a theater was the *orchestra,* the central acting area, which was surrounded three-quarters of the way by the seating area. At the open end of the orchestra stood the stage building or *skene,* where the actors could change and store their belongings. The first theaters were simple structures built on the natural slope of the hill and made of wood. In the fourth century B.C., the structures became permanent and were made of stone. Many of the stone theaters still stand today. The most famous theater is at Epidaurus, in the Peloponnese. It is still used today for the performance of ancient Greek plays.

Athletic competitions were the main attractions of other Greek festivals. The most prestigious of these festivals was the Olympic Games, held in honor of Zeus, the king of gods. The event took place every four years in the sanctuary of Zeus at Olympia, located in the northwest part of the Peloponnese. The sanctuary of Zeus was a sacred area dedicated to the god and his wife, Hera. After the Olympic Games were instituted in Zeus's honor, the sanctuary grew in size. Not only were temples and altars erected for the religious activities, but a stadium and hippodrome (a stadium designed for equestrian events) were constructed for the athletic events. In the beginning, athletes and spectators alike had to live uncomfortably in the open air. Buildings to accommodate the athletes and the spectators were absent until fairly late in the history of the sanctuary. In the fourth century B.C. a guest house, a gymnasium, and two bath houses were built to ease the comfort of the people and competitors. The Olympic Games first originated in 776 B.C. and are still celebrated today. Like all festivals, religious observances were a main part of the ceremony, which included sacrifices made to the honored god.

There were eight different types of athletic competitions that took place over a three-day period at the Olympic Games. The chariot races and the horse races were carried out in the hippodrome. The chariots had two wheels and were pulled by four horses. Crashes and fatalities were frequent during the chariot races. The remainder of the athletic events took place in the stadium. The stadium was about 200 meters long (600 feet) with the natural slopes of a hill serving as the seating area for the spectators and the judges. The events consisted of boxing, wrestling, the *pankration* (a mix of boxing, wrestling, and judo), track events, a race in armor, and the *pentathlon*. The pentathlon was a five-part contest that included the discus throw, the long jump, the javelin throw, a 200-meter run, and wrestling. The track events consisted of three running races: the 200 meter, the 400 meter, and a longer race of about 5,000 meters. The race in armor was the final athletic competition and demonstrates the importance of the hoplite (a type of heavily-armed soldier) in the Greek army.

There was only one winner for every contest. There were no second- and third-place winners. The winners of the various contests were rewarded with simple garlands of olive leaves, but the prestige associated with being an Olympic victor was great. At home, the victor might get some money prizes or free meals for the rest of his life. Sometimes statues of the victors were sculpted and displayed in public places. The victors were seen as heroes.

Other games were established in Greece, but none as prestigious as the Olympic Games. Two of these were the Pythian Games at Delphi, held every four years, and the Isthmian Games at Corinth, held every two years.

Many Greeks from far away places flocked to see the festivals. They were very religious people who did not want to anger the gods by not attending the festivals. At the same time, the festivals were social events that were not to be missed.

Name _____ Date _____

POINTS TO PONDER

1. What are some differences between Greek and modern theaters?

_____

_____

_____

_____

2. If you were a playwright, what themes that are relevant to the present day would you choose to write a Greek-style tragedy about?

_____

_____

_____

_____

3. What kind of people and ideas in our society would you make fun of in a comedy?

_____

_____

_____

_____

4. What are some differences between the Greek Olympic Games and the modern ones?

_____

_____

_____

_____

Name _____ Date _____

CHALLENGES

1. What were the two main functions of a Greek festival?

_____

_____

2. What two kinds of plays were written by Greek playwrights?

_____

3. Who were the three most famous Greek tragedians?

_____

4. Who was Aristophanes?

_____

5. What was the function of the chorus in Greek plays?

_____

_____

6. In honor of which god were the Olympic Games established?

_____

7. What is a hippodrome?

_____

8. What was the most prestigious festival in which athletic competitions took place in Greece?

_____

9. Name the athletic events that people enjoyed watching at the Olympic Games.

_____

_____

10. Name the three main parts of a Greek theater.

_____

11. Name the famous Greek tragedy written by Sophocles.

_____

12. Name the historical tragedy written by Aeschylus.

_____

THE ETRUSCANS AND THE BEGINNINGS OF ROME

This bronze wolf is thought to have been made by an Etruscan artist in about 500 B.C.

The peninsula of Italy was centrally located in the Mediterranean Sea and became the home of many peoples. It had fertile soil for cultivation as well as a pleasant climate and a variety of metal ores, such as copper and iron. Indo-European people migrated to Italy from the north in two successive waves. First, in about 2000 B.C. people who used bronze tools and weapons arrived. Then, about 1000 B.C. Iron Age people moved in, using superior iron tools and weapons. These were the ancestors of the different Italic tribes that inhabited most of Italy by the ninth century B.C. Most notable of the Italic tribes were the Latins who lived near Rome in the area called Latium. Between 750 and 600 B.C. the Greeks settled to the south of Rome in the area known as Magna Graecia. To the north of Rome, between the Tiber and Arno Rivers, the Etruscans settled (in the area known as Etruria). (See map on page 89.)

The Etruscans were self-governed and lived in this region from the eighth century B.C. until they were conquered by the Romans in the third century B.C. It is not known where the Etruscans came from. Some historians claim they migrated from Asia, while others claim they were native to Italy. It is known that they were not Indo-European, and they spoke an unknown language. The Etruscans have left behind numerous monuments and artifacts that attest to an advanced and flourishing civilization in pre-Roman Italy.

The Etruscans were organized into a confederation of twelve city-states, each with its own king. Some examples were Caere, Tarquinia, Chuisi, Populonia, Veii, and Volsinii. Volsinii was the religious center, and a religious festival was held there annually. The city-states were built on low hilltops surrounded by strong fortifications. An extensive road system connected the city-states.

The Etruscans were skilled bronze workers. They made bronze pots, tools, weapons, sculptures, and household items. In their artwork, they were greatly influenced by the Greeks in the south, who traded extensively with them. They also adopted the Greek alphabet to write their language and in turn passed it on to the Romans, who used it to write Latin.

Extensive *necropoli* (cemeteries) scattered the landscape. The Etruscans buried their dead in monumental tombs. These tombs consisted of rock-cut chambers that were often covered by a large *tumulus* (mound of earth). The local rock was called "tufa," a rock of volcanic origin that was very soft and easily cut. The Etruscans cut family tombs in the tufa cliffs that looked like the insides of their houses, with several chambers connected to a main chamber. On stone benches inside the chambers lay carved *sarcophagi* (stone caskets) in which the dead were laid to rest. In tombs found at Tarquinia, paintings with scenes of everyday life decorate the tombs and give valuable information to archaeologists.

37

When the Etruscans were conquered by the Romans, they started cremating their dead and putting the ashes in carved stone urns. On many sarcophagi and urns, portraits of the dead were sculpted in stone, and a carving of the dead person's name, family, and occupation was inscribed.

The Etruscans were at their height of power between the seventh and fifth centuries B.C. They expanded their territory beyond their homeland of Etruria to the north as far as Bologna and to the south into Campania. This included the settlement of Rome on the Tiber River. Rome was an aggregate of separate villages that had been united into one community by the mid-eighth century B.C. The inhabitants of Rome, who were Latins, lived in primitive huts made of thatch and mud. During the time of the Etruscan occupation, Rome grew into a city and flourished. A century later Rome took the lead and began, little by little, to take over all the peoples of Italy: the Italic tribes, the Greeks, and the Etruscans.

According to legend, Rome was founded by the twins, Romulus and Remus, in 753 B.C. Titius Livius (known as Livy) describes the events of the early history of Rome and its foundation. He tells how after the sack of Troy by the Greeks, a Trojan prince, Aeneas, sailed around the Mediterranean and eventually landed in Italy, where he settled. Aeneas married the daughter of King Latinus, the king of the Latins. After Aeneas's son founded a new city, Alba Longa (near Rome), he and his descendants ruled the city for thirteen generations until Amulius seized the throne from the real king, Numitor. Numitor had twin grandchildren, Romulus and Remus, whom a servant, on Amulius's orders, was supposed to drown in the Tiber River. Instead, the servant left the twins in a basket on the river bank. A she-wolf nursed them until a shepherd found and raised them. When the boys reached manhood, they took revenge upon Amulius and killed him. Together they founded a new city on the spot where they had been left behind as babies. After a quarrel, however, Romulus killed his brother and became the first king of the newly-founded city, which was named Rome after him. A bronze she-wolf from about 500 B.C., a masterpiece made by an Etruscan artist, can still be seen in Rome today.

Romulus was followed by six more kings. The fifth and seventh kings of Rome were Etruscan in origin. With the fifth king, Tarquinius Priscus, the period in which the Etruscans dominated Rome and the Latins began. During that time, Rome became a city surrounded by a defensive wall with a central marketplace (the Forum), public buildings, and temples. When Etruscan power began to decline in Latium and Campania during the sixth century B.C., the last king, Tarquinius Superbus, was expelled by the Roman aristocrats. The traditional date for the end of this period known as the "Monarchy," which began in 753 with the founding of Rome, is 509 B.C. This date (509 B.C.) also marks the beginning of Roman civilization.

The Etruscans are an important part of Roman history because the Romans adopted many customs from them. Examples include the arch and the layout of the temple in Roman architecture, the Etruscan alphabet (adopted from the Greeks) used to write Latin, the reading of the future by looking at the entrails of animals, the art of bronze making, and very importantly, some aspects of Roman government. The Romans were also influenced greatly by the Greek culture, which can be seen in their architecture, sculpture, science, and literature.

38

Name _____ Date _____

POINTS TO PONDER

1. To what extent did the Etruscans play a significant role in the development of Rome?

_____

_____

_____

_____

_____

2. What are the main features that characterize the Etruscan civilization?

_____

_____

_____

_____

_____

3. What is meant by the "Monarchy" of Rome? According to the legends, which events mark the beginning and end of this period?

_____

_____

_____

_____

_____

Name _____ Date _____

CHALLENGES

1. Which three peoples inhabited Italy by 700 B.C.?

_____

2. In which area did the Etruscans live?

_____

3. For what type of artwork were the Etruscans best known?

_____

4. Who was Romulus?

_____

_____

5. How did the Etruscans bury their dead?

_____

_____

6. Who raised the twin brothers Romulus and Remus?

_____

7. What customs did the Romans adopt from the Etruscans?

_____

_____

_____

8. What language did the Romans speak?

_____

9. In which areas did Greek culture influence Roman culture?

_____

10. How was the Etruscan civilization organized?

_____

_____

11. On which river was Rome located?

THE REPUBLIC OF ROME
PART 1: 509–218 B.C.

With the expulsion of the last king of Rome, a new period in Roman history started, and a new form of government replaced the monarchy. This period is called the Republic, a name given to the new state by the Romans.

The king was replaced by two men, called *consuls,* who held all the executive power. They also commanded the army in times of war. They were advised by a governing body of ex-magistrates, known as the *Senate.* This council originated during the Etruscan occupation of the city, when it served as an advisory body to the king. Officially, the responsibility of the Senate remained the same, but as Rome

This clay dish from Campania shows one of the war elephants of King Pyrrhus of Epirus.

grew in power it became a very influential body of government in regard to internal and foreign policy. The Senate controlled all matters of great importance, such as decisions of war. Other important positions within the government were the judge of the city *(praetor);* the financial officer *(quaestor);* the office of public relations *(aedile),* which organized festivals and other events; and the high priest *(pontifex maximus).* The Roman people were divided into two social classes: the *patricians,* who were the land-owning aristocracy, and the *plebeians* or the common people, who were farmers and traders. In the beginning, only the patricians could hold the offices of consul and be members of the Senate, so they controlled the government. It was also a Roman custom that the patricians become the protectors, or *patroni,* of some poorer people, ex-slaves, or newcomers to the city, who were known as *clientes.* The patroni helped the clientes financially and legally in return for help in their political and private lives. This custom of patron-client relationship helped the leading aristocratic families retain their influence in the state, both politically and socially.

Internally, during the Early Republic phase (509–133 B.C.), discontentment occurred among the plebeians because they were not allowed to participate in the government, and the little land they owned was slowly being taken by the patricians. This left the plebians in a state of debt and servitude, which led to a social struggle between the two classes lasting over 200 years. It was a bloodless revolution, however. By means of strikes and refusing to perform their duties to the state, they sought social and political equality. Little by little the plebeians were given certain rights. Every year elections were held for two men, called "tribunes of the people" (known as *tribuni plebis*), who would represent the people in government affairs. The laws of Rome were published on twelve stone tablets and displayed in the Forum. Gradually plebeians were allowed to enter positions in the government. Finally, a law was passed in 287 B.C. known as the *Lex Hortensia,* in which a People's Assembly was officially recognized. This plebeian assembly had the force of the law. It could pass or veto any law that was put before it and make decisions on matters of the state. In theory, the people had the power, but in practice, it was the Senate who decided the complex and significant matters of the state. This led to more strife between the two classes and eventually to civil war during the second phase of the Republic period (133–30 B.C.)

Externally, during the first three centuries of the Republic, Rome grew to be a world power. With an efficient army and notable leaders, Rome expanded her domain throughout Italy and the Mediterranean. (See inset map on page 89.) Until 300 B.C. the Romans fought the neighboring mountain tribes known as the Volsci, the Aequi, and the Sabini. In 390 B.C. Rome drove off the Gauls who had invaded from the north across the Alps and had ravaged and burnt the city of Rome. Over the next century the Etruscans of the north and the Latin tribes of Latium were conquered. During the last thirty years of the fourth century, the Samnites were the enemy. The Samnites, who dominated Campania, were the toughest Italic tribe the Romans had to face, but in a series of three wars, the Samnites were finally defeated. By 280 B.C. Rome dominated central and northern Italy. The only people left to conquer in Italy were the Greeks who lived in the south. For fear of a Roman invasion, the Greeks of the city of Tarentum asked for help from their countrymen on the Greek mainland. In 280 B.C. King Pyrrhus of Epirus crossed the Adriatic Sea, landed in Italy, and fought the Romans for five years. The war against the Greeks was called the Pyrrhic war, after the Greek king. Pyrrhus was a tough enemy to defeat because he used elephants in his battles against the Romans. At first, he was successful, because the Romans had never seen elephants before and were scared. But eventually the Roman army was able to deal with the elephants and defeated Phyrrus in 275 B.C. Pyrrhus withdrew back to Epirus in Greece. By 272 B.C. Tarentum and all the other Greek city-states in Italy had submitted to Rome. Rome made separate alliances with each of the conquered cities. As allies, the cities were independent, but had to supply the Romans with men for their army.

In the third century B.C. the Romans were at war with Carthage, the remaining prominent power in the western Mediterranean. Carthage, located on the coast of North Africa, was a colony established by the Phoenicians, a seafaring people from the Syrian coast (present-day Lebanon). The Phoenicians had dominated the western Mediterranean Sea since the ninth century B.C. and had founded many colonies along the Mediterranean coast. Carthage was the most important of these. Within a century, Carthage controlled the North African and Spanish coasts, Sardinia, Corsica, and western Sicily. Rome fought three wars with Carthage. These were called the Punic Wars (Punic is Latin for Phoenician).

The First Punic War (264–241 B.C.) broke out because of a conflict of interest over Sicily. Fighting was harsh on both land and sea, but the Roman army was strong. Carthage lost, and a truce was made between the two powers. Rome acquired Sicily and Sardinia and these islands together became the first province of Rome. A province was controlled by a Roman magistrate, who set up a local government and collected taxes to be paid to Rome. Carthage, however, would not give up. After the First Punic War, the Carthaginians occupied Spain to replace the island territories they had lost. Another clash between Carthage and Rome became inevitable in 218 B.C., when a Carthaginian general sought revenge for his country. The provocation was a conflict about the possession of the Spanish town of Saguntum. The Second Punic War is discussed in the next chapter.

Name _____ Date _____

POINTS TO PONDER

1. Who, in theory, was in control of the Roman state under the Republican type of government? In reality, who had the power in the Roman state and why?

_____

_____

_____

_____

_____

2. Trace the three different phases of Roman territorial expansion throughout Italy. Who were the enemies the Romans had to fight?

_____

_____

_____

_____

_____

3. What was the reason for the social struggle between the plebeians and the patricians during the Early Republic?

_____

_____

_____

_____

_____

Name _____ Date _____

CHALLENGES

1. What was the function of the Senate?

_____

_____

2. Who were the consuls?

_____

3. Who were the patricians?

_____

4. Who were the plebeians?

_____

5. What was the Lex Hortensia?

_____

_____

6. What was Rome's first province?

_____

7. Who was Pyrrhus of Epirus?

_____

_____

8. Why are the wars with Carthage called the Punic Wars?

_____

9. Name five important offices of the Republican government.

_____

_____

_____

10. What was a Roman province?

_____

THE REPUBLIC OF ROME PART 2: HANNIBAL 218–133 B.C.

The Carthaginian general who was involved in the events leading up to the Second Punic War (218–201 B.C.) was Hannibal. He is considered to be one of the ablest and most brilliant generals the Romans ever faced.

Hannibal decided to lead his army, which included elephants, into Italy from the north. (See map on page 90.) He crossed the high, snow-covered Alps with difficulty and lost more than half of his elephants and soldiers. Despite his many losses, Hannibal was victorious over the Romans during the first two years of the war. His army forces were not as numerous as those of the Romans, but his generalship and new battle tactics won him a series of battles. The

These coins depict Hannibal of Carthage and one of his war elephants.

last and greatest victory for Hannibal was at the Battle of Cannae in 216 B.C. In this battle a whole Roman army was destroyed.

The Romans refused to admit defeat, however. New and more capable generals were chosen to fight the Carthaginians. One such general was Cornelius Scipio. While Hannibal remained in Italy waiting for reinforcements to arrive in Spain, an army under Scipio fought the Carthaginian army in Spain. The Romans also prevented Hannibal from receiving any reinforcements by killing his brother in battle. Scipio, adopting Hannibal's battle strategy, drove the Carthaginians out of Spain in 206 B.C. From Spain, Scipio proceeded to invade Africa and attacked the city of Carthage itself. This move forced Hannibal to leave Italy and meet Scipio in a battle in his home territory. The battle took place in 202 B.C. at Zama, where Scipio won a great and final victory over Hannibal. After this victory, Scipio became known a Scipio Africanus and the defeated Hannibal fled to Asia. A peace agreement between the Carthaginians and the Romans was signed in 201 B.C. Carthaginian might was destroyed, and Spain was made into two Roman provinces. The Romans became the leading power of the western Mediterranean.

Rome now focused its attention on the eastern Mediterranean, and her sea empire grew larger. In the first century B.C., she became involved in wars with Macedonia, Greece, and Syria. In 168 B.C. the Kingdom of Macedonia was seized. Greece became part of the Roman Empire in 146 B.C. after a revolt in the city of Corinth was crushed. That same year Carthage was razed to the ground at the end of the Third Punic War. Macedonia and Greece became one Roman province, and Carthage formed the province of Africa. In 133 B.C. King Attalus of Pergamon in Asia died and left his kingdom to the Romans. This became the province of Asia. Hence, by 133 B.C. Rome had established seven provinces on three continents along the Mediterranean: Sicily and Sardinia (one province), Corsica, Spain (two provinces), Africa, Macedonia-Greece, and Asia.

Name _____ Date _____

POINTS TO PONDER

1. What were the reasons for the eventual and final Roman victory over Carthage and its general, Hannibal?

_____

_____

_____

_____

_____

_____

_____

_____

2. Trace Roman territorial expansion from the end of the First Punic War to 133 B.C. Name the seven provinces the Romans had acquired.

_____

_____

_____

_____

_____

_____

_____

_____

Name _____ Date _____

CHALLENGES

1. Who was Hannibal?

_____

_____

2. Who was Scipio?

_____

_____

3. Whose battle strategy did Scipio adopt?

_____

4. Which battle was the greatest victory for Hannibal?

_____

5. Which battle was the greatest defeat for Hannibal?

_____

6. Which provinces did the Romans acquire after the Second Punic War?

_____

7. By 133 B.C. how many provinces of Rome were there? How many continents did the provinces cover?

_____

_____

8. In 146 B.C., which two Roman provinces were created?

_____

9. In which war were the generals Hannibal and Scipio involved?

_____

10. In which war did the city of Carthage join the Roman sea empire?

_____

11. How did the Romans gain the province of Asia?

_____

_____

THE REPUBLIC OF ROME
PART 3: CIVIL WARS
133–46 B.C.

The war with Hannibal had harmful effects on the political situation in Rome and Italy. Much of the farmland was left in ruins, having been plundered by Hannibal's troops and abandoned by its owners, who had to serve in the Roman army. As a result, many of the soldier-farmers were left without property, became unemployed and poor, and moved to the big cities. The state bought up the small farms and leased them to the wealthy upper class. Farms became larger, and products such as olives and grapes were cultivated on a large scale for commercial purposes. This trend only increased the gap between the rich and the poor. The Senate, which consisted of the wealthy landowners, also remained in full control of the state. The Republic's constitution was not in the hands of the people as designed. This led to unrest among the people. Reforms were needed to prevent anarchy from breaking out.

Gnaeus Pompeius Magnus, known as Pompey, led the Roman army in victorious campaigns in Spain, Bythinia, Syria, and Judaea.

Social reforms were proposed to the Assembly of the People in 133 B.C. by Tiberius Gracchus, a tribune of the people. This action, which was in accordance with the Lex Hortensia, was bitterly opposed by the Senate. The reforms included a law setting a maximum amount of property each individual could hold. It also allowed for the redistribution of land to the poor citizens of Rome. Tiberius was trying to reinstall the small landholders in Italy and take care of urban poverty. However, the members of the Senate did not wish to lose their property or their power. They reacted violently by killing Tiberius before the reforms could be carried out. The assassination of Tiberius by the Senate proved to be damaging and is considered the turning point in the history of the Roman Republic. It was the beginning of the decline and fall of the Republic.

Ten years later, the brother of Tiberius, Gaius Gracchus, attempted to pass the same laws that his brother had proposed. His attempt failed because he was also killed by the Senate. For another century, the struggle between the people, who sought more power, and the aristocracy, who fought to keep their power, continued. Each faction was led by men who tried to rebuild the shattered Republican constitution. The leaders were distinguished generals who had proven their worth in wars in Europe and Asia. But political and personal rivalry between the leaders became common. Social disorder and civil wars resulted.

In 107 B.C. Gaius Marius came to power as consul of Rome. He created a professional Roman army by allowing the poor citizens from the cities to join the army for terms of 16 years. In return, the soldiers would be rewarded with a piece of land to settle on once their military service was finished. This military reform was instrumental to the rise of powerful generals because the army became more loyal to its generals than to the state. While Marius was fighting the Gauls, barbarians who inhabited the area north of Italy and much of western Europe, his lieutenant, Cornelius Sulla, became a powerful general. In

88 B.C. Rome was facing a rebellion in Asia Minor that required Roman intervention. The people wanted Marius to lead the war, but instead, the Senate chose Sulla, who had become a consul. As a result, Sulla marched on Rome and declared Marius an outlaw. Marius fled to Africa, and Sulla went to the east to deal with the rebellion. As soon as Sulla left for Asia Minor, however, Marius and his supporters took control of Rome once again. Marius died in 86 B.C., but his followers continued the battle. In 82 B.C., on his way back from the east, Sulla again marched on Rome with his army, and the first civil war broke out. The two forces, Marius' followers supported by the people and Sulla's troops supported by the Senate, met in a battle outside Rome. Sulla was victorious and declared himself dictator of Rome. He was put in charge to restore the old Republican constitution and did so by restoring much of the Senate's power in the government and breaking the power of the people. In 80 B.C. he resigned from his dictatorship; he died the following year.

The new power of the Senate did not last long. Two brilliant generals, Pompeius Magnus, known as Pompey, and Crassus, became powerful leaders. Pompey had increased his military reputation with victorious campaigns in Spain. Crassus was put in command of the Roman army to repress a slave rebellion led by a professional gladiator, Spartacus, in southern Italy. After two years of fighting, Crassus was able to capture Spartacus with the help of Pompey, who had just returned from Spain. Spartacus was killed, and thousands of his fellow slaves were crucified. Pompey and Crassus decided to run together for the consulship of Rome in 70 B.C.

During their consulship, they overturned Sulla's laws and restored the power to the people, thus weakening the power of the Senate. The conflicts between the Senate and the people resumed. While Crassus stayed in Rome, Pompey continued to increase his military reputation in campaigns in the east. He expanded Rome's territories by combining Pontus and Bythinia into the Roman province of Bythinia in 68 B.C. He defeated the last king of the Seleucid Empire in Syria in 63 B.C. and enlarged the province of Asia. Lastly, the kingdom of Judaea in Palestine became a client state of Rome.

While Pompey was in the east, Gaius Julius Caesar became popular in Rome through his victories in Spain. Trouble was also brewing in Rome—a conspiracy in 63 B.C. led by Cateline almost overthrew the state. The Senate increasingly insulted Pompey, Crassus, and Caesar with the result that they joined forces to form a coalition, called the *First Triumvirate* (60–53 B.C.), in which all three men shared the power of the state. The growing ambitions of the leaders, who commanded their own armies, soon led to another civil war, however. Caesar had just finished the conquest of Gaul (58–51 B.C.). Fearing the power of Caesar, Pompey forced him to disarm his troops and accept humiliation before returning to Rome. But Caesar did not wish to give up everything for which he had fought, so he and his army crossed into Italy, starting the second civil war (49–46 B.C.). Due to his brilliant generalship and speed of movement, Caesar won a series of major battles against Pompey's forces, defeating Pompey himself in 48 B.C. at the Battle of Pharsalus in Greece. (See map on page 90.) After defeating Pompey's sons and other Pompeian supporters in Africa and Spain in 46 B.C., Caesar became sole ruler of the Republic and was appointed dictator of Rome for life.

Name _____ Date _____

POINTS TO PONDER

1. What two major effects did the Punic Wars have on the political situation in Rome? What was the long-term result?

_____

_____

_____

_____

_____

2. What kind of social reforms did Tiberius and Gaius Gracchus try to make and why? Why did their attempts fail?

_____

_____

_____

_____

_____

3. Describe the political situation in Rome in the first century B.C. Why did several rival generals rise to power in Rome?

_____

_____

_____

_____

Name _____ Date _____

CHALLENGES

1. Who were Tiberius and Gaius Gracchus?

_____

_____

2. What was the purpose of the Gracchi brothers' reforms?

_____

_____

3. Which influential reform is attributed to Gaius Marius?

_____

4. Who was Sulla?

_____

5. Who were the two principal leaders during the second civil war?

_____

6. Who was Pompey?

_____

7. Who was Spartacus?

_____

8. What was the First Triumvirate?

_____

_____

9. In which battle was Pompey defeated?

_____

10. Why did civil wars occur in Rome during the first century B.C.?

_____

_____

11. Which two factions, led by powerful leaders, were involved in the civil wars?

_____

THE REPUBLIC OF ROME PART 4: JULIUS CAESAR

Julius Caesar (100–44 B.C.) can be considered one of the best military commanders of all time. His most significant accomplishment was the conquest of Gaul. The annexation of Gaul changed the whole concept and character of the Roman state. Roman civilization now incorporated not only the lands around the Mediterranean but also western Europe. (See map on page 90.)

Gaul was made up of a number of Celtic tribes. In 58 B.C. during the First Triumvirate, Caesar became governor of the provinces of Cisalpine Gaul (northern Italy), Illyricum (east of the Adriatic Sea), and Narbonese Gaul (southern France). He decided to march northwards and make the whole area into a Roman province, because he claimed that the tribes posed a threat to the Gallic provinces. Some maintain, however, that his attack on the Gauls was

Gaius Julius Caesar was a member of the First Triumvirate with Pompey and Crassus, but he soon eliminated his co-rulers and in 46 B.C. became sole dictator of Rome for life.

due to his own ambition and desire to increase his military prestige. So started the "Gallic War" (58–51 B.C.). The account of the war was reported by Julius Caesar himself in his book *De Bello Gallico.*

After the Gallic War, Caesar became involved in the civil war against Pompey, whom he defeated in Greece in 48 B.C. In 47 B.C. Caesar went to Egypt where he met Cleopatra, and they became lovers. After Caesar helped her defeat the king of Egypt, he made Cleopatra queen of the land. Egypt also became a client state of Rome. Then Caesar returned to Italy, where he was made dictator of Rome for life in 46 B.C.

During his dictatorship, Caesar accomplished much and devoted his career to reforms. One of his most important reforms was the establishment of colonies in Italy and the provinces to deal with the ongoing problem of the urban poor and the landless ex-soldiers. The colonies were small settlements for war veterans intended as a reward for their loyalty. Civilians, specifically the unemployed poor of the cities, were also allowed to live there. The colonies became important places of defense and acted as instruments in the Romanization of the provinces. Caesar also tackled the long-standing problem of debt. He erected a number of public buildings in Rome. He also revised the Roman calendar, which, with minor changes, is still used today.

Due to the nature of his reforms, Caesar incurred the hostility of the upper class and the Senate. A conspiracy against him was planned and instigated by two leading members of the Senate, Cassius and Marcus Brutus. Eventually there were sixty conspirators. The murder happened when the Senate gathered for a meeting in Pompey's theater. There the conspirators cruelly stabbed Caesar to death. Caesar died on the Ides of March (March 15), 44 B.C.

Name _____ Date _____

POINTS TO PONDER

1. What do you think was Julius Caesar's most significant accomplishment before he became dictator of Rome? Why?

_____

_____

_____

_____

2. What were Julius Caesar's accomplishments as dictator? Which of these do you think was most significant?

_____

_____

_____

_____

3. Why do you think Caesar was murdered by members of the Senate?

_____

_____

_____

_____

Name _____ Date _____

CHALLENGES

1. Who was Julius Caesar?

_____

_____

2. Which region did Caesar annex to the Roman state?

_____

3. Why did Caesar decide to march against the Gauls?

_____

_____

4. What was the reason given by Caesar's critics for his conquest of Gaul?

_____

_____

5. Which Roman leader did Caesar fight during the civil war?

_____

6. Who did Caesar make queen of Egypt?

_____

7. Which of Caesar's reforms is still used today?

_____

8. Who murdered Caesar?

_____

9. On which day was Caesar murdered?

_____

10. What was the function of a colony?

_____

_____

_____

OCTAVIAN-AUGUSTUS: THE FIRST ROMAN EMPEROR

After Caesar's death, his right-hand man, Mark Antony, tried to gain control of the situation. At the same time, Octavian, who was the grand-nephew and adopted heir of Caesar, also rose to power with the support of the Senate. In 43 B.C. both generals and one of Caesar's military commanders, Lepidus, established the second Republican coalition of three dictators to rule the Roman state. This was called the *Second Triumvirate.*

Both Antony and Octavian proceeded to fight Caesar's murderers, Brutus and Cassius, and defeated them in 42 B.C. in two battles at Philippi in Macedonia. It was then decided by both leaders that Antony would control the eastern provinces and Octavian would control the western provinces.

Octavian defeated Mark Antony at the Battle of Actium and became the sole ruler of the Republic. He was later granted the title, Augustus, and became the first emperor of the Roman Empire.

Soon tension between the two men started to grow because Antony had abandoned his wife, who was Octavian's sister, and was having an affair with Queen Cleopatra of Egypt. Jealousy and ambition were also factors in forcing the two dictators apart. About the same time, the third dictator, Lepidus, contested Octavian's supremacy in the West and, as a result, was forced to retire and was disarmed. As the years went by, the rivalry between Antony and Octavian increased until the third and final civil war of the Republic broke out. In 31 B.C. Octavian defeated Antony and his ally, Cleopatra, at the Battle of Actium on the west coast of Greece. Both Antony and Cleopatra fled to Egypt where they committed suicide. Octavian, in turn, conquered Egypt in 30 B.C. and made it a Roman province. (See map on page 90.)

After the Battle of Actium, Octavian became the sole ruler of the Republic. He planned to restore Rome to its old glory and establish peace and stability after a century of war. In order to accomplish his goal, however, he had to form a new type of government that resembled the old Republic constitution but did not include its weaknesses. Learning from his predecessors' mistakes, he did not make himself a dictator. Instead, for his first years in power, he concealed his power behind republican traditions. In 27 B.C. he pronounced "the transfer of the state to the free disposal of the Senate and the people." This action earned him the reputation of being the restorer of the Republic, whereupon the Senate bestowed on him the title of AUGUSTUS (which means "the revered one") to define his new status as leader of the Roman state. He was known as Augustus thereafter. Augustus became the first emperor of the Roman Empire, which lasted from 27 B.C. to A.D. 476.

Thus, the outcome of the Battle of Actium was three-fold: (1) It was the end of the Roman Republic; (2) Octavian-Augustus became the master of the Graeco-Roman world; and (3) The Roman state was dominated by the West with Rome as the capital, while the East was kept in second place.

Even though Augustus retained many of the republican offices, such as the consulship and the Senate, he was the supreme ruler of the state. He embodied the roles of the president of the Senate, leader of the Roman army, and chief priest. He was granted power over the senatorial governors in the provinces and power as the tribune of the people. The courts, legislation, finance, and internal and foreign policy were all in his hands.

Augustus took extensive journeys and reorganized the Roman provinces. He made Egypt into a Roman province. He added the whole Iberian Peninsula (Spain and Portugal) to the empire, and he made Gaul into three new provinces. In the east he annexed Galatia in Asia Minor and made Judaea into a Roman province. Augustus's stepson, Tiberius, campaigned north of Italy and managed to extend the Roman territories to the Danube and Rhine Rivers, making the rivers the natural furthermost boundaries of the Roman Empire. (See map on page 90.)

Augustus accomplished other deeds as well. He created a permanent bodyguard and a city police, which were stationed in Rome. He instituted a fire brigade. He founded a new military treasury from which he could pay his soldiers. He also embellished Rome with a number of public buildings, both restoring old ones and erecting new ones. This greatly pleased the people of Rome.

Augustus showed himself to be a great general and administrator in the reorganization of the government and the provinces. He transformed the shattered Republic into a new regime that was to last for many centuries. He solved the problem of governing by making the Roman state a one-man rule, accomplished in the appearance of the old republican traditions. He created a durable Roman peace, called the *Pax Romana,* that lasted for two centuries, until A.D. 180. During this period there was no major war and the economy prospered. An extensive network of roads extending throughout the empire increased the flow of trade. Trade flourished in exports such as wool, olive oil, wine, metal work, and pottery. In return, Italy received goods from the provinces, including slaves, grain, marble, and ivory. Production from agricultural goods, rather than trade, however, provided the major part of Rome's total revenue.

A year before Augustus died, he made a will that included a summary of the military and financial resources of the empire and a political testament of his achievements. This testament is called the "Res Gestae Divi Augusti" or "Acts of Achievement of the Divine Augustus" and provides historians with an important document of Augustus's life and accomplishments.

To ensure that the rule of the empire stayed in the hands of men of his choice, Augustus arranged his own successors to the throne by adopting them as his sons. As the years went by, he chose several candidates, but they either died in battle or were poisoned to death. When Augustus died, the only remaining candidate, his stepson Tiberius, succeeded him as the next emperor.

Augustus ruled Rome for 44 years and died in A.D. 14. For the next half century, the empire was ruled by four members of Augustus's family, known as the Julio-Claudian Dynasty. Augustus's successor was Tiberius (14–37). Then Caligula (37–41), Claudius (41–54), and finally, Nero (54–68) succeeded to the throne.

Name _____ Date _____

POINTS TO PONDER

1. How did Octavian, unlike his predecessors, manage to become sole ruler and first emperor of the Roman world?

_____

_____

_____

_____

_____

2. Do you think that Octavian deserved the title of "Augustus"? Why?

_____

_____

_____

_____

_____

3. What is meant by the *Pax Romana*? Why was this term used to describe the first two centuries of the history of the Roman Empire?

_____

_____

_____

_____

_____

Name _____ Date _____

CHALLENGES

1. In which battles were Caesar's murderers defeated?

_____

2. Who was the first emperor of the Roman Empire?

_____

3. Which two leaders were involved in the third civil war?

_____

4. Which battle ended the third civil war?

_____

5. What is the "Res Gestae Divi Augusti"?

_____

_____

6. What does *Pax Romana* mean?

_____

7. Who succeeded Augustus as emperor?

_____

8. Why was Octavian given the title "Augustus"?

_____

_____

9. What was the significance of the Battle of Actium?

_____

_____

_____

_____

10. Which two rivers formed the furthermost boundary of the Roman Empire in Europe during the reign of Augustus?

_____

NOTABLE EMPERORS: THE EARLY ROMAN EMPIRE
A.D. 14–180

Nero was the last emperor of the Julio-Claudian Dynasty. He was such a bad ruler that finally his own army killed him.

The last two emperors of the Julio-Claudian Dynasty were notable for their actions. Claudius (A.D. 41–54) was known for his activities in the provinces. He was responsible for incorporating Britain as a province into the Roman Empire. Mauritania, in Africa, and Thrace, north of Greece, were also added as Roman provinces during his reign. (See map on page 90.) Claudius adopted his stepson, Nero, to succeed him on the throne.

Nero (54–68) is considered one of the worst emperors to rule Rome. Upon his accession to the throne, he quickly lost interest in public affairs. He preferred to be involved in pleasure activities such as music, drama, races, and sexual activities. His rule is also known as the "reign of terror," because he suspected many members of the Senate of conspiracy and put them to death. Nero even killed some members of his own family, including his mother. In A.D. 64 a great fire swept through Rome. Nero blamed the small Christian community for the fire. As a result, many of the Christians were persecuted and killed. It was thought, however, that Nero himself had planned the fire. In fact, right after the fire had destroyed much of the city, he started building a new imperial palace that was decorated with gold. It was called the "Golden House" and extended over a large part of the city. Nero's unpopularity increased in the last years of his reign when he started appearing in public performances. He went on an artistic tour of Greece where he participated in many of the games, winning all the first-place prizes. Finally, the army, neglected by the emperor, killed him.

Following Nero's murder, revolts led by different Roman armies broke out in the provinces. This led to a short period of civil war (68–69) in which four emperors ruled the state. The last of the four emperors, Vespasian, brought stability back to the empire.

Vespasian, succeeded by his two sons, Titus and Domitian, belonged to the Flavian Dynasty of rulers (69–96). Vespasian and Titus ruled the empire well. A Jewish revolt in Judaea was suppressed in A.D. 70 with the capture and destruction of Jerusalem. Both emperors concentrated on the reconstruction of the empire and strengthening its defenses. In Rome, a lot of money was spent on public works—most notably the Colosseum, which was a large arena where gladiatorial fights were held. One noted event during the short reign of Titus was the eruption of the volcano Vesuvius, near Naples in A.D. 79. Ash from the volcano buried two nearby towns, Pompeii and Herculaneum, and wiped out most of the population. Vespasian's other son, Domitian, was not a popular ruler. He was a second Nero. He ruled the empire with a stiff hand, neglecting the Senate. This caused dissatisfaction among the Senate's members. Afraid for his life, Domitian put many of the Senate's leading members to death. His unpopularity cost him his life at the hands of a member of his bodyguard and his own wife.

59

The next century was dominated by the "Five Good Emperors." This period of the second century A.D. was considered the "Golden Age" of the Roman Empire. Most notable of the five emperors were Trajan (98–117), Hadrian (117–138), and Marcus Aurelius (161–180).

Trajan came from Spain and was the first emperor to come from a province. This symbolized the start of provincial men rising to power within the ruling classes of Rome. Trajan was popular with both the Senate and the people. Even though he had absolute control of the state, he put on a good show towards the Senate with his diplomacy. He is best remembered for his military conquests and public works in Rome and the provinces. Trajan conquered a region called Dacia, north of the Danube River, and annexed it to the empire. He also fought the Parthians in the east and annexed Armenia, Mesopotamia, and part of Arabia to the Roman Empire. No emperor had gone this far and none would go beyond. The Roman Empire, in terms of territorial expansion, reached its largest extent during Trajan's reign. (See map on page 90.) Trajan's many public works, paid for by the booty from Dacia, adorned Rome and the provinces. One of these was the Column of Trajan in Rome, around which the story of Trajan's achievements in Dacia was carved in a spiral decoration. Trajan's good rule in Rome and abroad earned him the title of "Optimus Princeps" or "Best Ruler."

Hadrian succeeded Trajan as emperor. Hadrian dealt extensively with troubles within the provinces. In fact, he spent more than half his reign outside of Rome, traveling throughout the provinces. Because the provinces of the east, newly-acquired by Trajan, were difficult to hold and defend, Hadrian abandoned them and withdrew back to the Euphrates River as the eastern boundary of the Roman Empire. Hadrian also strengthened the Roman boundaries in the west by building defensive walls along the Rhine and Danube Rivers as well as a wall in Britain, which was named after him. Hadrian's Wall marked the northernmost extent of Roman occupation in Britain and the empire as a whole. Hadrian's main goal was to stabilize the Roman Empire. He is also known for the construction of public buildings in the provinces as well as a private palace surrounded by gardens and pools in Tivoli, just outside Rome.

Marcus Aurelius was the last of the "Five Good Emperors," and his death brought an end to the Pax Romana created by Augustus. He was known as the "philosopher-king," because he was deeply involved with philosophical thoughts that he wrote down in a book called "Meditations." During most of his reign, Marcus Aurelius was involved in the defense of the Roman Empire, fighting against the Parthians in the east and the German tribes who started to break through the frontier along the Danube River. (See map on page 90.) In addition, a plague struck the empire, killing many civilians and soldiers. The loss of life caused by wars and natural disasters resulted in a man shortage. This led to large numbers of Germans being admitted into the empire as settlers and auxiliary soldiers along the boundaries. These Germans helped the Romans in the defense of the empire against other German tribes who started to threaten the frontiers on a larger scale. In addition to the man shortage, the wars were costly and resulted in financial problems. Defending the borders of the empire, not the conquest of additional territory, now became the primary concern for the emperor and his Roman army. This meant more money was being spent than was coming into the empire. Thus, ecomonic as well as political stability began to decline in the Roman Empire.

Name _____ Date _____

POINTS TO PONDER

1. Which of the emperors during the early Roman Empire were unpopular and as a result were murdered? Why?

_____

_____

_____

_____

_____

2. Why was the second century A.D. regarded as the "Golden Age" of the Roman Empire?

_____

_____

_____

_____

_____

3. Which of the "Five Good Emperors" do you think accomplished the most during his reign and why?

_____

_____

_____

_____

_____

Name _____ Date _____

CHALLENGES

1. Who conquered Britain?

_____

2. Who was blamed for the Great Fire of Rome in A.D. 64?

_____

3. Whose reign was called the "reign of terror"?

_____

4. Name the volcano that erupted in A.D. 79, burying the towns of Pompeii and Herculaneum.

_____

5. In whose reign did the Roman Empire reach its greatest extent territorially?

_____

6. Who built a defensive wall in Britian that was named after him?

_____

7. Which areas did Trajan conquer and temporarily add to the Roman Empire?

_____

_____

8. Which emperor was known as the "philosopher-king"?

_____

9. Why was Nero's palace called the "Golden House"?

_____

_____

10. What was carved on the Column of Trajan?

_____

_____

NOTABLE EMPERORS: THE LATE ROMAN EMPIRE
A.D. 180–305

Marcus Aurelius was succeeded by his son, Commodus (180–192). Commodus was another emperor like Nero. He is regarded as one of the most eccentric of Rome's emperors because he was addicted to emotional religions and gladiatorial sports. His relations with the Senate were hostile, and this led him to execute many of its members. Finally, the head guard of the imperial bodyguard commissioned a professional athlete to murder him.

After a period of civil war following the death of Commodus, Septimius Severus became emperor.

As happened after Nero's death, a civil war followed for four years (193–197). In 193 a rich senator and two provincial governors were all hailed as the emperor of Rome at the same time. Eventually, Septimius Severus from North Africa, who was the provincial governor in the Danube region, defeated his rivals and became the sole emperor (193–211). Septimius Severus made a number of significant changes in the governmental structure to secure the position of the emperor and prevent disorder and rebellion within the state. In Rome, he excluded the remaining senators from his administrative positions and filled them with knights of purely military training. As a result, the so-called sharing of power between the Senate and emperor was now entirely gone. He also replaced the imperial bodyguard with his own Danubian soldiers and doubled its size.

During this time the defense of the Roman Empire became a bigger and graver problem than before. Septimius Severus added more provincial natives as soldiers to the army, increasing its size. He also initiated steps to make the officers of the army a privileged social class. He increased their pay and rewards by increasing the taxes on civilians. These changes indicate that the army had become the sole basis of the emperor's power. Septimius Severus died in Britain while on a military campaign in 211. On his deathbed, he advised his sons to "be on good terms with one another, be generous to the soldiers and don't care about anything else." Septimius left the empire jointly to his two sons, Geta and Caracalla. Until 235, Septimius Severus and his successors continued to deal with the increasing problems along the frontiers of the empire.

Military anarchy followed for a period of 50 years (235–284). This is called the period of "barrack emperors." A series of soldier emperors who were appointed and then overthrown by different provincial armies came to the throne. Along with the 27 "regular" emperors, there were about 50 military usurpers who assumed the imperial title. Rome now faced its most serious problem: the appointment of the emperors by the armies. The loyalty of the soldiers had shifted towards their generals rather than the state. Above all, greed was the motive for frequently changing emperors. The more gifts and rewards an emperor could distribute, the more loyalty the soldiers showed.

63

During this 50-year period, the situation along the frontiers deteriorated. Invasions of Germanic tribes along the northern border and the new Persian Sassanid Empire along the eastern border posed an increasing threat to the empire. As a result, the Romans abandoned Dacia, and the boundary was brought back to the Danube River. (See maps on pages 90 and 91.) Both the internal wars and frontier battles had a lasting effect on Rome's stability.

By 284, within fifteen years, the military situation had recovered and the empire was temporarily restored. However, the economy within the empire had collapsed. The imperial treasury was depleted, old taxes were increased, new taxes were raised, and inflation was at an all-time high. Moreover, trade declined, and Rome became entirely dependent on imported goods from the east, hardly exporting any goods of its own. Many farms were abandoned, and on the farms where production of goods continued, there was no increase in productivity because there was no technological improvement. Rome's social situation also collapsed due to a decline in population. The middle class disappeared and lower-class farmers suffered tremendously.

The emperor who came to power after this 50-year period of civil war was Diocletian (284–305). He was temporarily able to restore a measure of stability to the empire. Diocletian was the greatest imperial organizer since Augustus. He tried to deal with the deteriorating military and economic situation of the Roman Empire by introducing a number of reforms.

In order to deal with the military situation, which was impossible for one emperor to handle, as well as to insure an orderly series of imperial successions, Diocletian partitioned the empire into a government ruled by four people. This was known as the *tetrarchy*. He appointed a second ruler as co-emperor of the state and two Caesars as secondary emperors who would succeed the emperors upon their deaths. Diocletian and his Caesar, Galerius, ruled the eastern half of the empire, and Maximian and his Caesar, Constantius, ruled the western half. Diocletian also reorganized the empire by increasing the number of provinces from 50 to 100, making them smaller in size with each under a provincial governor. The provinces were grouped into thirteen major units, called *dioceses,* each ruled by governors. In turn, the dioceses were grouped under four *prefectures,* each under an administrator called a prefect. (See map on page 91.) In doing so, he made the governing of the empire more efficient and insured little opportunity for internal revolts. Diocletian also restructured the Roman army by creating two branches: a mobile field force and a frontier force.

In an attempt to restore the economic situation, Diocletian issued an edict of prices that fixed the maximum prices on all goods and transportation costs, as well as the maximum wages for all workers throughout the empire. He made an attempt to stabilize the coinage and made the process of tax collecting more systematic. However, he was not able to lessen the burden of taxation on the Roman people because he needed the money to carry out his reforms.

To sum up, Diocletian created a totalitarian state in order to maintain the imperial defenses and stop economic decline. The Senate had disappeared. In 305 Diocletian stepped down from his throne due to health reasons, and he forced Maximian to do the same. Galerius and Constantius became co-emperors in their place.

Name _____ Date _____

POINTS TO PONDER

1. Why does the year 180 mark the end of the Pax Romana (Roman Peace)?

_____

_____

_____

_____

_____

2. What type of change did Septimius Severus make in the structure of the Roman government? Why did he make this change, and what effect did it have on the position of the emperor?

_____

_____

_____

_____

_____

3. To what extent do you think Diocletian's reforms reversed the economic and political decline of the Roman Empire?

_____

_____

_____

_____

_____

Name _____ Date _____

CHALLENGES

1. Describe the period of the "barrack emperors."

_____

_____

2. Who made the army the basis of the emperor's power?

_____

3. Who was Commodus?

_____

4. Who tried to restore the economic and political situation of the empire after the 50-year period of civil war?

_____

5. What was the tetrarchy?

_____

_____

6. What were the names of the two new administrative units of the Roman Empire that Diocletian instituted?

_____

7. What was the edict of prices?

_____

_____

8. What did Septimius Severus say to his two sons on his deathbed?

_____

_____

9. What was the relationship between the emperor and the Senate during the late Roman Empire?

_____

10. What military reform did Diocletian make to deal with the threatening situation along the frontiers?

_____

THE RISE AND SPREAD OF CHRISTIANITY

Christianity originated in the eastern Roman Empire in the first century A.D. It began as a sect of Judaism in Palestine, in the Roman province of Judaea, with the birth and death of Jesus. The life and teachings of Jesus would alter the course of western history. For two centuries, Christianity spread slowly throughout the Roman Empire. The early spread of Christianity can be largely attributed to Paul, a Jew from the Greek city of Tarsus in Asia Minor. During the first half of the first century, Paul traveled throughout the eastern part of the empire spreading the gospel of Jesus.

Later, through other people's missionary work, Christianity spread throughout the rest of the Roman world. It was first adopted among the urban-dwellers in the big cities of the empire, including Rome. During the third century, Christian communities throughout the empire grew at a rapid rate due to the insecurities of the time. The people of the Roman Empire had lost faith in the state and were seeking individual

Constantine legalized Christianity throughout the Roman Empire and was himself baptized a Christian on his deathbed.

and personal salvation. To satisfy this religious quest, the people turned to the sacramental religion of Christianity. Christianity was also popular because it offered the emotional satisfaction of religious love and preached the equality of all people. It was a literate religion that accepted Classical culture and, as a result, also attracted the educated members of the empire.

The official religion of the Roman Empire was the Roman state religion, which, like the Greeks', involved the worship of many gods. It was a *polytheistic* religion and is known as *paganism*. The Romans also worshipped the emperor as a god. The Roman state tolerated any religion that did not threaten the tranquility and safety of the empire. As long as the people participated in the worship of the emperor and the state religion, the Roman state did not interfere in their private lives. The Christians, however, refused to worship the Roman gods and the emperor. As a result, during the first three centuries A.D., the Christians were regarded as traitors and were persecuted by the Roman emperors.

Persecutions of Christians had started under Nero, when they were blamed for the big fire of Rome that occurred in A.D. 64. They continued to be carried out on a small scale by Domitian, Marcus Aurelius, and Septimius Severus. The persecution culminated in the reigns of Diocletian and Galerius, between 303 and 311. This was known as the "Great Persecution of Christians." Then, in 311 Galerius issued the Edict of Sophia, an edict of tolerance in favor of Christianity. Christianity was legalized in the eastern half of the Roman Empire.

After the resignation of Diocletian and Maximian, the planned succession of the tetrarchy broke down in confusion. By 310, there were five emperors ruling the Roman Empire. Among the rulers was Constantine the Great (306–337) who eventually emerged as the sole ruler of the empire. Constantine had succeeded Constantius in 306 as ruler of

67

the western half of the empire. Constantine defeated, one by one, the other rival emperors. In 312 he defeated Maxentius in the Battle of the Milvian Bridge in Rome and became sole ruler of the western half of the empire. At this battle, Constantine asserted that his victory over Maxentius was due to a miracle. According to his biographer, Eusebius, just before the battle Constantine saw a flaring cross in the sky and the following inscription: BY THIS SIGN THOU SHALT CONQUER. The sign was the Christian XP (Chi-Rho) sign, which he put on the shields of his soldiers. In this way, Constantine became the first Christian emperor of the Roman Empire, although he was not baptized until the moment of his death. In 324 Constantine defeated his remaining rival in the East, Licinius, and became the sole ruler of the Roman Empire. (See map on page 91.)

During his reign, Constantine the Great initiated a series of measures favoring the Christians. In 313 he issued the Edict of Milan, which legalized Christianity throughout the empire. He exempted Christian clergy from any secular obligations, such as paying taxes. Imperial funds were used to subsidize the building of churches in the provinces. In addition, Constantine took steps to defend Christianity by taking actions against current heresies that had emerged. In the fourth century, separate movements within Christianity developed due to disputes and controversies in the doctrines of the Christian belief; most notable of these was *Arianism*. Arianism was founded by Arius, an Egyptian priest from Alexandria who disputed the positions of the three individuals of the Trinity (God the Father, the Son, and the Holy Spirit). Arius and his followers believed that the three individuals of the Trinity were not equal, unlike the Christian belief. In 325 Constantine tried to resolve the dispute by calling a meeting of church leaders at the Council of Nicaea. This meeting produced the Nicene Creed, which declared Arianism a heresy. In short, Constantine was responsible for the conversion of the empire from paganism to Christianity.

In regard to the domestic affairs of the empire, Constantine continued to carry out the reforms begun by Diocletian. He tightened control of the empire and increased taxation. He continued to reorganize the army by increasing the proportion of German troops and elevating them to high positions. When Rome was no longer capable of serving as the capital of the Roman Empire due to its distant location from the boundaries, Constantine founded a new capital. He built the new capital on the Greek town of Byzantium, located on the Bosporus Strait, and renamed it Constantinople (present-day Istanbul). Constantinople was ideally located to supervise both the northern-Danube and eastern-Euphrates defenses.

Christianity continued to flourish under Constantine's successors. In the reign of Theodosius I (378–395), Christianity took another important step forward. Theodosius became known as "the Great" because he insisted on the rigorous practice of Christian orthodoxy. He suppressed any remnant of paganism and Arianism, and by the end of his reign (394), Christianity was made the official religion of the Roman Empire.

Christianity was one of the most important Roman legacies to Western civilization.

Name _____ Date _____

POINTS TO PONDER

1. Why did Christianity spread so rapidly throughout the Roman Empire and eventually become the official Roman state religion?

_____

_____

_____

_____

_____

2. Why do you think Christianity is regarded as the most important of Roman legacies to Western civilization?

_____

_____

_____

_____

_____

3. The Romans tolerated other religions as long as they did not endanger the state. Why did they react so violently toward Christians?

_____

_____

_____

_____

_____

Name _____ Date _____

CHALLENGES

1. Where did Christianity originate?

_____

2. What is meant by a polytheistic religion?

_____

3. What was the Roman state religion called?

_____

4. What is the Edict of Sophia?

_____

_____

5. Who was the first Christian emperor of the Roman world?

_____

6. Who made Christianity the official state religion of the Roman Empire?

_____

7. Name the edict that legalized Christianity throughout the Roman Empire.

_____

8. Who was Arius?

_____

9. What was Arianism?

_____

_____

10. At which battle did Constantine the Great see the XP sign in the sky?

_____

THE FALL OF THE ROMAN EMPIRE A.D. 337–476

After the reign of Constantine, the Roman Empire declined rapidly. After the reign of Theodosius in 395, the empire was permanently split into two parts, the western half and the eastern half, each with a different emperor who acted independently from the other. (See map on page 91.) When historians talk of the fall of the Roman Empire, they only mean the western half of the empire. The Western Roman Empire held on for less than a century until its collapse in the fifth century. The Eastern Roman Empire survived for a thousand years longer and was known thereafter as the Byzantine Empire.

The immediate cause for the fall of the Western Roman Empire was the Germanic invasions across the Roman frontiers. The Romans had continuously battled Germanic tribes for some time. However, during the fourth and fifth centuries, the Germans started to cross the borders and invade the empire on a massive scale. (See map on page 92.)

Attila the Hun's invasion of Gaul and Italy failed; however, the movement of the Huns triggered invasions of Germanic tribes that eventually toppled the Roman Empire.

The Germans were a loosely-knit group of people, organized into a number of different tribes that the Romans had to fight individually. Along the Rhine River, the Franks, the Vandals, and the Burgundians threatened the empire's borders. Along the Danube River, the Goths posed a dangerous threat to the empire. The Goths were divided into two states, the Ostrogoths (eastern Goths) and the Visigoths (western Goths).

The massive Germanic invasions were triggered by the movement of another tribe of barbarians, called the Huns, who probably lived in northern China. By 370 the Huns had moved west into the Balkan area and entered the Danube River basin, conquering the Ostrogoths along the way. As a result, the Visigoths were terrified and were driven across the Danube River into the Roman Empire where they settled in 376.

Because of their unjust treatment at the hands of the Romans, the Visigoths revolted and ravaged northern Greece. In 378 the Roman emperor, Valens, dealt with the crisis and met them in a battle at Adrianople, in Thrace. For the first time, the Roman army was defeated by a Germanic tribe, and Valens was killed. This battle is regarded as one of the worst defeats the Roman army ever experienced. The Battle of Adrianople was a decisive battle because it marks the beginning of Germanic invasions into the Roman Empire on a massive scale. It also showed the Germans that the Roman army was not invincible.

After the battle, the Visigoths were pacified and were allowed to settle within the borders of the Roman Empire living under their own leaders. Under their leader, Alaric, the Visigoths moved west and invaded Italy several times and finally sacked Rome in 410. The Visigoths eventually moved to Spain where they set up their own kingdom in 418.

While dealing with the Visigoths in 406, the Roman army had to abandon both the Rhine River and British frontiers. This left the borders open, and the Vandals, the

Burgundians, and the Franks invaded the empire, plundering many Roman towns along the way. At first, the Romans made a treaty with the different Germanic tribes and granted them "federal" status within the empire. This meant that they were allowed to live under their own rulers, but had to supply the Romans with soldiers and farmers. They became allied to the Romans. Eventually, the different tribes openly ruled their own states and tore themselves away from Roman control. The Vandals moved into Spain and then Africa, where they set up their own kingdom in 439. The Burgundians settled along the Rhone River in southern Gaul in the 430s. The Franks inhabited northern Gaul and unified into the Frankish kingdom in 481.

In the meantime, the Romans also had to deal with the Huns, who had become another threat to the empire. By the early fifth century, the Huns had built up an empire from the Baltic Sea to the Danube River. In 434 Attila became their leader. He ruled for 19 years and was known as the "Scourge of God" because he played a large part in the downfall of the Western Roman Empire. In 451 Attila marched into Gaul where he met a combined army of Romans and federate Germans in a battle at Chalons on the Marne River. Attila was defeated, and he had to evacuate Gaul. However, in the following year Attila decided to cross the Alps into Italy and attack Rome. His plan failed, and Attila withdrew from Italy. In 453 he died, and his empire fell apart.

By the middle of the fifth century, the Western Roman Empire was coming to an end. For the last twenty years, the empire was ruled by many emperors who had become mere puppets on the throne. Their election depended solely on powerful German generals in the army. Finally, in 476 the last emperor of the Roman West, Romulus Augustulus, was overthrown by a German general called Odovacar. Odovacar was proclaimed King of Italy by his soldiers. Italy became the last Germanic kingdom. Several Germanic kingdoms in the west and the Byzantine Empire in the east replaced what once was the mighty Roman Empire.

The Roman army, superior in numbers and equipment, had dealt with the Germans for a long time, defeating them in many battles over the years. Why then were the barbarian invasions in the fifth century successful in destroying the Western Roman Empire? The underlying causes had their roots in the late Roman Empire. Politically, there was internal disunity. One of the prime causes of disunity was the failure of emperors to control the army and its generals, which led to numerous civil wars. The emperors were not able to secure peaceful succession to the throne. As a result, the emperors could not successfully defend the imperial borders. In addition, because of the man shortage in the army, more and more Germans were recruited as soldiers and generals. These German recruits proved to be less dependable and loyal to the Roman state than Roman soldiers. Economically, the Roman Empire was drained. During the last three centuries of rule, the prime concern of the emperors was the defense of the Roman frontiers rather than expansion. This meant that more and more was spent on the army while less and less money was coming into the empire. Taxes continued to increase, which resulted in the rise of inflation. The stagnation of technology and decrease in trade were also major factors in the decline of Roman power. All these factors affected the empire socially. The people became poorer and dissatisfied, which destroyed individual loyalty toward the Roman state. The Germanic invasions of the fourth and fifth centuries merely sped up the process of collapse in the Western Roman Empire.

Name _____ Date _____

POINTS TO PONDER

1. Why were the Romans not able to defeat the Germans in the fifth century despite their superiority in numbers and equipment?

_____

_____

_____

_____

2. Do you think that the Western Roman Empire would have lasted longer if the German invasions had not posed a threat to the empire? Why?

_____

_____

_____

_____

3. Who succeeded the Romans in the Mediterranean after the collapse of the Western Roman Empire in the fifth century?

_____

_____

_____

_____

4. Some historians believe that the rise and spread of Christianity may have been a factor in the fall of the Western Roman Empire. Can you find some reasons why this may have been the case?

_____

_____

_____

_____

Name _____ Date _____

CHALLENGES

1. In which battle did Valens fight the Visigoths?

_____

2. Which barbarian movement started the massive Germanic invasions across the Roman frontiers?

_____

3. In which battle did the Romans defeat the Huns in 451?

_____

4. Who was Attila?

_____

_____

5. Why was the Battle of Adrianople a decisive battle?

_____

_____

_____

6. Name the Germanic tribes that lived beyond the northern borders of the Roman Empire and eventually invaded the empire.

_____

_____

7. Who was the last emperor of the Roman West?

_____

8. Who deposed the last emperor of the Roman West?

_____

9. What was the new name for the Eastern Roman Empire?

_____

10. What battle in 378 was regarded as one of Rome's worst defeats?

_____

ROMAN ARCHITECTURE

The surviving architecture in Rome today is testimony to its grandeur in the days when it was the capital of the Roman Empire. Rome, located on the Tiber River and surrounded by seven hills that provide a naturally protected site, controlled the whole Mediterranean world for many centuries.

The buildings that embellished Rome at the peak of its power during the Imperial period were numerous and impressive. These included theaters, baths, temples, libraries, imperial palaces, basilicas or public meeting places, fora (plural of forum) or commercial and social centers of the city, and arenas for public events. Public monu-

The forum was the chief marketplace of Rome. It also contained temples, basilicas, the Senate House, and public monuments to the emperors.

ments commemorating the achievements of emperors, such as triumphal arches and columns, were also erected. Bridges, aqueducts (artificial channeling systems for conducting water to the city), and a strong defensive wall with access gates completed the array of public structures that once adorned the city of Rome. These types of monuments and structures could be found in any Roman city throughout the empire.

The nucleus of a Roman city was the *forum,* an area of open space that served as the commercial and social center where people met to socialize and businesses sold their goods. Lawcourts were also located there. A forum consisted of a central, open, rectangular space surrounded by basilicas, which were long, open structures supported by columns, and a temple. The greatest and oldest forum in the Roman world was the Forum Romanum, the chief marketplace of Rome. It was unusual in that it was not built in one phase, but grew in size through the years. It was filled with basilicas, temples, the Senate House, and the triumphal arch of Septimius Severus.

The Romans adopted several architectural features from the Etruscans and the Greeks. They adopted the form of the arch from the Etruscans. From the Greeks, they used the classical orders of the Greek temple, most commonly the Corinthian architectural order. The Romans developed and combined these elements with a new type of building material, concrete, to form their own unique architectural style.

During the Late Republic period, the Romans invented a new building material that we still use today. By mixing volcanic dust and lime mortar, they produced a cement that hardened into concrete. The Romans used it as the core for the walls of buildings. Because concrete was unattractive to the eye, they faced it with marble slabs or baked clay bricks. The many surviving Roman monuments throughout western Europe testify to the strength and durability of concrete.

The Romans made great use of the Etruscan arch. The Etruscans used it as a single stone structure to build gateways in their fortification walls. But the Romans used the arch in various ways, and in combination with the use of concrete, created architectural structures of great size and strength. They created the *vault* by putting a series of arches side by side. A *dome* was created by several arches crossing in different directions in a circular space that intersected in the center. The use of arches and concrete revolutionized Roman architecture. New ways of exploiting the interior space of buildings were developed, thus creating monuments of great size and complexity.

There are many examples of these arch structures in Rome and the provinces. The most simple use of the arch can be seen in the construction of city gates, bridges, and aqueducts. Bridges consisted of a series of arches joined in a line and were built across valleys and rivers. Many are still in use today. An aqueduct consisted of one to three levels of joining arches through which water was channeled into a city. Vaulted arches were used in the construction of triumphal arches commemorating the achievements of the Roman emperors. The walls were carved with sculpted reliefs of the emperors' triumphs, sacrifices, and battles. Corinthian columns also decorated the outside of the archways.

Arches and Greek columns were also used in the construction of theaters and ampitheaters (round theaters). The most famous example of such a monument was the Colosseum in Rome. Arches were used throughout the building to support the different levels of the seating area. The outer facade consisted of three stories of arches, decorated with Greek columns in between each of the arches. Arches, vaults, and domes were used in the construction of the imperial palaces and public buildings, such as baths, to create vast interior spaces.

The Greek influence in Roman architecture can be seen in the form of columns on the outer facades of the aforementioned monuments, but it can most easily be noticed in the construction of basilicas and temples with the use of Corinthian-style columns. A basilica was a long portico supported by a series of columns. It served as an open-air, public meeting place. A typical Roman temple consisted of a closed structure built on a high platform. The temple structure, in most cases, had a deep, columned porch in the front. Sometimes, it was surrounded entirely by columns, as in a Greek temple.

One of the most impressive and fully-preserved examples of the Roman ability to exploit interior space in conjunction with the use of Greek columns was the Pantheon. The Pantheon, built by Hadrian, was a temple dedicated to all gods. The building was made of solid concrete and consisted of a round main room topped by a dome. It was fronted by a porch of Corinthian columns. The interior of the temple was lavishly painted and decorated with gold.

The private dwellings of the Romans were of two types. The common people lived in tightly-packed apartment buildings, much like today. The wealthier Romans built large townhouses, furnished with numerous rooms and a garden. The center of the typical Roman house was the *atrium* or living room, which was surrounded by the other rooms of the house. These included the kitchen, bedrooms, dining room, and store rooms. At the end of the house was a small garden. Because the houses had very few and small windows, the sloping roof of the houses had a hole right above the center of the atrium, called the *compluvium,* where light and air could enter. The rain water would be collected below in a pool, called the *impluvium,* which was the same size as the hole. It was common for two rooms in the front of the house on either side of the main entrance and fronting the street to be used as shops. The Romans decorated their houses with elaborate frescoes depicting scenes of everyday life.

EXAMPLES OF THE ARCHITECTURE
OF THE ROMAN EMPIRE

Roman Bridge

Roman Aqueduct

Roman Triumphal Arch

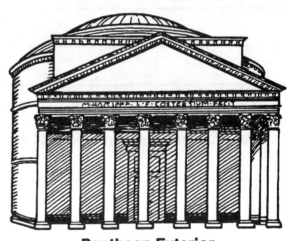

Pantheon Exterior

Roman Townhouse

Pantheon Interior

Name _____ Date _____

POINTS TO PONDER

1. To what extent was Roman architecture influenced by the Etruscan and Greek civilizations?

_____

_____

_____

_____

2. What Roman inventions revolutionized Roman architecture?

_____

_____

_____

3. What kinds of monuments did the Romans build?

_____

_____

_____

4. Describe a typical townhouse owned by a wealthy Roman.

_____

_____

_____

_____

Name _____ Date _____

CHALLENGES

1. What was the forum?

_____

_____

2. What was the function of an aqueduct?

_____

3. Which architectural feature did the Romans adopt from the Etruscans?

_____

4. What is Roman concrete?

_____

_____

5. What is the Pantheon?

_____

_____

6. Which architectural feature did the Romans adopt from the Greeks?

_____

7. What was the central feature of a Roman townhouse?

_____

8. How is a dome built?

_____

_____

_____

9. What is a vault?

_____

10. What was the impluvium?

_____

ENTERTAINMENT

Many grisly events were held for the entertainment of the Roman people in the Colosseum. Built in the reigns of Vespasian and his sons, the Colosseum was a building of tiered arches that supported seating areas for 45,000–55,000 people. Below the center stage of the structure were underground rooms and cages where wild beasts and the participants of the events were kept before the games began. There was also a water system that allowed for the flooding of the stadium in order to carry out mock sea battles.

Romans looking for entertainment could go to the Colosseum where events such as gladiatorial fights and mock sea battles were held.

One of the main events held in the Colosseum was the hand-to-hand combat between gladiators. Gladiatorial fights were first performed among the Etruscans and were, as blood sacrifices, part of a religious ritual at funerals. The Romans took over this gruesome contest as entertainment for the people. It became an important way for Roman emperors to control the people by satisfying their lust for action and bloodshed. At the start of the fights, the gladiators shouted together to the Roman emperor: "We who are about to die salute you." Then the fights began. Gladiators fought each other until one of them was killed. Sometimes, however, a gladiator would not kill his opponent, but only wound him. If a victim fell wounded, he could ask for mercy from the emperor. The emperor would listen to the pleas of the crowd and decide the fate of the victim with a signal of his thumb. If the emperor gave the thumbs-up sign, the victim lived. If he pointed the thumb downward, the victim would be killed.

More cruel than the duels between gladiators were the executions of criminals by wild beasts. These were also held in the Colosseum. Unarmed, helpless human beings were thrown to wild lions and bears. When the Christians were persecuted during the reigns of Nero, Domitian, and Diocletian, they were also thrown to the wild beasts.

Chariot races were another popular event held in Rome to appease the populace. Chariot races were held at the Circus Maximus, a 700-yard-long oval stadium that could hold about 150,000 people. The chariots were drawn by two, three, or four horses. Even though these races were not as gruesome as the gladiatorial fights, crashes were common, and some charioteers were trampled to death by approaching horses and chariots.

Another form of recreation involved the Roman baths, called *thermae,* which were not just places to cleanse oneself, but were also places for social gatherings. Wealthy Romans often spent whole days at the baths. The Romans did not use soap to wash themselves, like today. Instead their bodies were rubbed with oil. The oil with the dirt was then scraped off with a *strigil,* which was a blunt razor-like tool. Men and women alike spent the day being bathed by slaves, exercising, discussing news, and playing games with their friends. A Roman bath house was a large structure with a changing room, a swimming pool, and four different kinds of baths: a cold room, a warm room, a hot room, and a dry sweating room. The baths were heated by steam from an underfloor heating system, called a *hypocaust.* By the Imperial period, the more elaborate bath houses included libraries, art galleries, shops, gymnasiums or exercise areas, and gardens.

80

Name _____ Date _____

POINTS TO PONDER

1. Do you think it is fair to say that the Roman civilization was a morally corrupt society? Why or why not?

_____

_____

_____

_____

2. Why did the emperors think it was important to provide entertainment for the people?

_____

_____

_____

_____

3. How were the Roman baths like the health spas of today? How were they different?

_____

_____

_____

_____

Name _____ Date _____

CHALLENGES

1. What was the Colosseum?

_____

_____

2. Where did the chariot races take place?

_____

3. Where did the gladiatorial fights take place?

_____

4. What did the thumbs-down sign mean?

_____

_____

5. What did the gladiators shout to the emperor before the fights began?

_____

6. How were the Christians persecuted?

_____

_____

_____

7. What was the original function of gladiatorial contests?

_____

_____

8. What is a hypocaust?

_____

9. What were the tools used by the Romans to clean their bodies?

_____

10. Name the four types of baths in a Roman bath house.

_____

_____

THE ROMAN ARMY

The Romans were able to conquer most of the ancient world and control vast territories and peoples for nearly a thousand years by means of its basic fighting force, the army. The army was the force behind the growth and greatness of Rome.

During most of the Republic period, before the first century B.C., the Roman army was recruited from the citizen body in times of war. The citizens were grouped into units of one hundred men each, called *centuries*. The army was organized according to social and economic classes. The wealth of each man determined in which century he fought. The wealthiest citizens served in the cavalry, because they could afford the full armor, whereas the poorest citizen, not being able to afford much protection, made up the light-armed troops. In the first century B.C., the consul Marius reorganized the Roman army by making it a professional army. All citizens, especially the poor and unemployed, were able to join the army for a wage and become professional soldiers, serving the Roman state for 16 years. Marius's military reforms made the army more flexible and interchangeable, eliminating the earlier army division according to economic and social classes.

A Roman soldier was armed with a short sword, a dagger, and a javelin. He was protected by armor, a helmet, and a shield.

The professional Roman army was an organized body of soldiers and officers that was divided into several units. The largest unit of the Roman infantry was the *legion*, which numbered between 4,000 and 6,000 men. The legion was divided into ten *cohorts*. Each cohort was divided into six *centuries*. Sixty centuries made up a legion. The Roman legions varied in number between 28 and 33 during the Imperial period.

The commander in chief of all legions was the *imperator*, who was also the emperor during the Imperial period. Each legion was commanded by a *legatus*, or commanding general, who was helped by six *tribuni*. The backbone of the legion was the *centurion*, who commanded the centuries (60 in number). Other officers included the second-in-command of the centurion, the standard-bearer, and the *tessarius*, who was responsible for the watchword.

The legions were drawn up for battle in a three-line formation. The first line consisted of young soldiers (*hastati*), the second line consisted of experienced soldiers (*principes*), and the third line was made up of veteran soldiers (*triarii*). Each was armed with a sword and spear for close-range combat. Every legion also had its own corps of specialists and its own cavalry. The cavalry was an auxiliary unit of the Roman army. The corps of specialists included writers, accountants, engineers, carpenters, and surveyors. These men were used to build roads and bridges, select the camps, and do the accounts.

The *auxilia*, or auxiliary army units, consisted of the light-armed troops and the cavalry. Men in the auxilia were recruited primarily from the provinces. The auxilia were divided into cohorts of 500 or 1,000 men each, which in turn were divided into centuries.

These forces supported the legions in battle. The auxiliary infantry unit was used to fight in front of the legions and used similar weapons as the legionary soldier. It also included soldiers with special functions such as archers or slingers. On the flanks of the legions fought the cavalry cohorts, consisting of about 120 men, called *alae* or wings. The auxiliary forces also served on the frontiers patrolling and defending the empire's borders.

During the Imperial period, a Roman soldier served in the army for 20 years. Life in the army was hard and busy. The soldiers were either fighting or training. The pay was little, and each soldier had to pay for his own food and clothing. The meals were rudimentary and consisted of porridge, bread, cheese, beans, and wine. The uniform of the legionary soldier was a linen vest over a woolen tunic. Over these garments was metal body armor. He wore a brown cloak that could be used as a blanket during cold periods. Sandals with hobnails were worn on the feet. A helmet and a large shield protected him on the battle field. The weapons used for fighting were a short sword, a dagger, and a javelin. At the end of his service, each soldier received a retirement payment and a plot of land, usually in colonies along the frontiers, where he was still called upon for duty to defend the empire in times of trouble.

The Romans were invincible for a long time, not only because of their trained and organized army, but also because of the siege weapons that they used in siege warfare. Mobile towers, ramps, and scaling ladders were used to besiege a city. The most impressive machine of all was the catapult, called the *ballista,* which hurled rocks and flaring darts against the enemy.

The Roman army set up temporary camps during campaigns. Camp was set up in a square area that was surrounded by a ditch. Behind this a mound and a rampart were built. On top of the rampart stood a palisade. Two main streets ran north-south and east-west through the camp. The commanding general's quarters were at the center of the camp, known as the *praetorium.* Other quarters included the soldier's barracks, the paymaster's quarters where prisoners, hostages, and booty were kept, and a forum that was the center of camp life.

Along the frontiers in the provinces, permanent camps, called *castra,* were set up. They were similar in plan to the temporary camps but permanent buildings were used. In addition to the soldiers' barracks, the general's quarters, and paymaster's quarters, the castrum included a hospital, storerooms, and baths.

During the late Imperial period when defending the frontiers rather than expanding the empire became the sole concern of the emperors, home recruitment began to decline. Emperors increasingly enrolled provincials and Germans, who had settled within Rome's borders, in the legions. By the time of Diocletian's reign, the previously unparalleled efficiency of the Roman legion was gone. In order to deal with the threatening situation along the borders, Diocletian and later Constantine changed the structure of the Roman army. The army was divided into two major branches: a mobile field force, consisting mostly of a cavalry, and a frontier force, which was permanently stationed along the border fortifications.

By the fifth century A.D., the Roman army was no longer able to stop the barbarian hordes from invading, and the Roman Empire collapsed.

Name _____ Date _____

POINTS TO PONDER

1. Discuss the development and organization of the Roman legion.

_____

_____

_____

_____

_____

2. Why was the Roman army able to conquer and control such a large area and its people for nearly a thousand years?

_____

_____

_____

_____

_____

3. Describe what you think a day in the life of a Roman legionary soldier would be like.

_____

_____

_____

_____

_____

Name _____ Date _____

CHALLENGES

1. What was the name of the largest unit of the Roman army?

_____

2. What was the name of the smallest unit of the Roman army?

_____

3. Who made the Roman army a professional body of soldiers?

_____

4. What is a cohort?

_____

5. Who was the imperator?

_____

6. Who were the auxilia of the Roman army?

_____

_____

7. Describe the uniform of a Roman legionary soldier.

_____

_____

8. What was a ballista?

_____

_____

9. What is a castrum (singular for castra)?

_____

_____

10. What kind of people made up the corps of specialists in the Roman army?

_____

_____

_____

Name_____ Date _____

Ancient Greece

BLACK SEA

Massalia

Byzantium

Cumae
Phaestum
MAGNA GRAECIA
SICILY

Athens

Syracusa

NEAR
EAST

MEDITERRANEAN SEA

EGYPT

Area of Greek
Colonization

Area of Original
Greek Settlement

MACEDONIA

Aegospotami

Hellespont
Troy

ASIA MINOR

AEGEAN
SEA

THESSALY

PERSIAN EMPIRE

Thermopylae

Artemision

Phocaea

Chaeronea
Delphi

Chalcis
Eretria

EUBOEA

IONIA

Thebes

Leuctra
BOEOTIA

Plataea

Marathon

Mycale

Corinth

Athens

ATTICA

Olympia

Mantinea

Salamis
Epidaurus

Miletus

Mycenae

PELOPONNESE

MESSENIA
Sparta

LACONIA

Thera

MEDITERRANEAN SEA

CRETE
Knossos

✠ Battle Sites

Name_____ Date _____

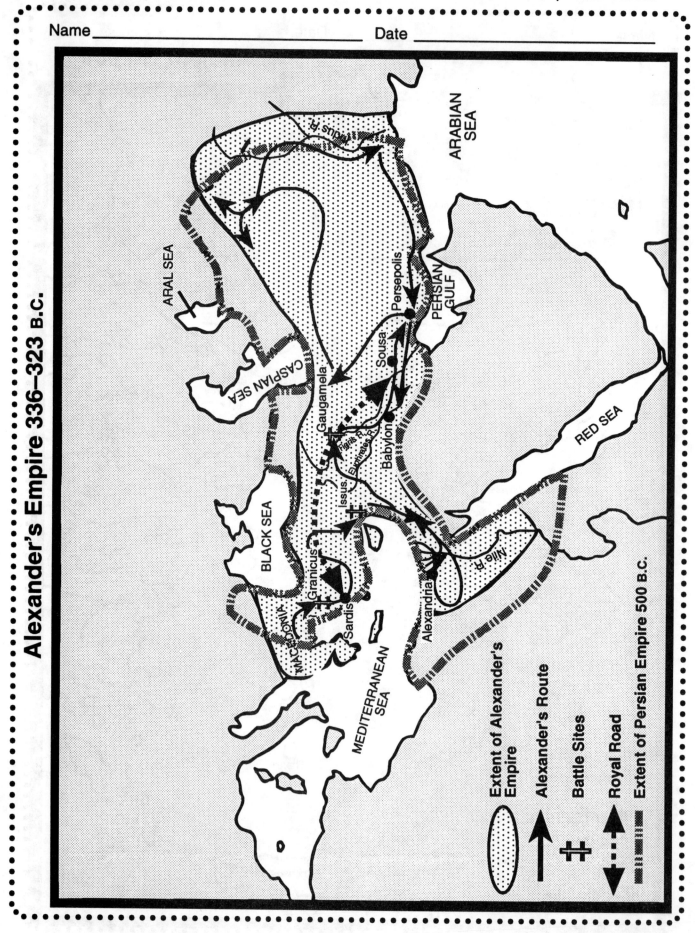

Alexander's Empire 336–323 B.C.

ARABIAN SEA

ARAL SEA

CASPIAN SEA

Indus R.

Persepolis

PERSIAN GULF

Sousa

Gaugamela

Tigris R.

Euphrates R.

Babylon

RED SEA

BLACK SEA

Issus

Granicus

Sardis

MACEDONIA

Nile R.

Alexandria

MEDITERRANEAN SEA

Extent of Alexander's Empire

Alexander's Route

Battle Sites

Royal Road

Extent of Persian Empire 500 B.C.

Italy and the Roman World 218 B.C.

Name_____ Date _____

MAP OF MEDITERRANEAN 218 B.C.

SPAIN

CORSICA

SARDINIA

Rome

EPIRUS

Carthage

AFRICA

SICILY

|||| Territories under Carthage's control

/// Territories under Rome's control

ALPS

Po River

Bologna

Arno River

Populonia

ELBA

ETRURIA

Tarquinia

Caere

Veii

Alba Longa

LATIUM

CORSICA

SARDINIA

TYRRHENIAN SEA

Chuisi

SABINES

AEQUI

Tiber River

Rome

LATINS

VOLSCI

SAMNITES

CAMPANIA

ADRIATIC SEA

Tarentum

MAGNA GRAECIA

SICILY

Territories under Rome's control 280 B.C.

Territory added 280–275 B.C.

Territory added 275–218 B.C.

Name _____   Date _____

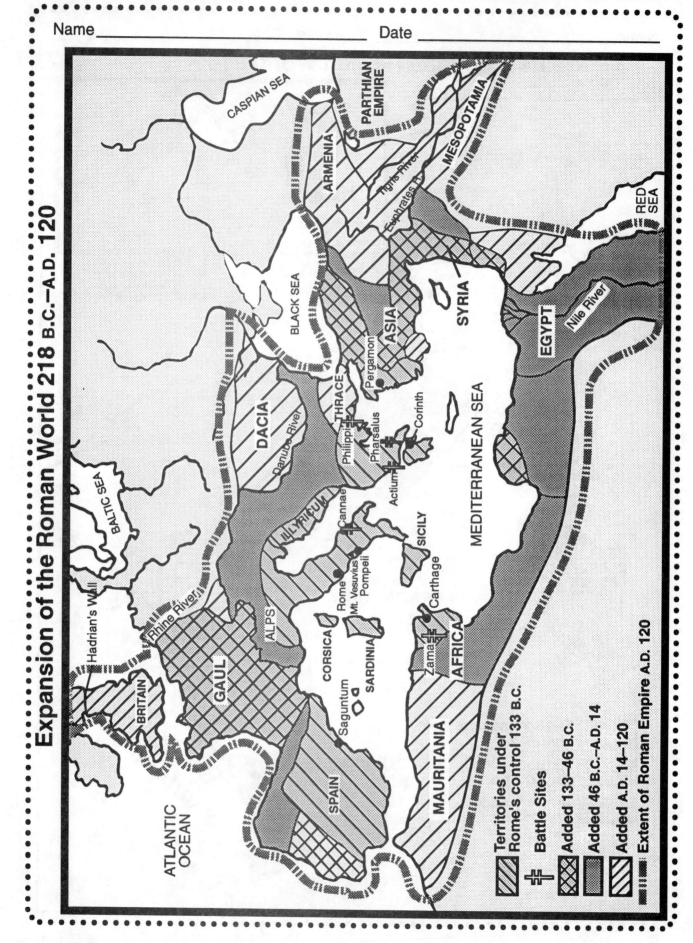

Expansion of the Roman World 218 B.C.–A.D. 120

CASPIAN SEA

PARTHIAN EMPIRE

ARMENIA

MESOPOTAMIA

Tigris River

Euphrates R.

RED SEA

BLACK SEA

SYRIA

ASIA

EGYPT

Nile River

Pergamon

DACIA

Danube River

THRACE

Philippi

Pharsalus

Corinth

Actium

MEDITERRANEAN SEA

BALTIC SEA

ILLYRICUM

Cannae

SICILY

Carthage

Hadrian's Wall

Rhine River

BRITAIN

GAUL

ALPS

CORSICA

Rome

Mt. Vesuvius

Pompeii

SARDINIA

Zama

AFRICA

Saguntum

SPAIN

MAURITANIA

ATLANTIC OCEAN

Territories under Rome's control 133 B.C.

Battle Sites

Added 133–46 B.C.

Added 46 B.C.–A.D. 14

Added A.D. 14–120

Extent of Roman Empire A.D. 120

Name_____ Date_____

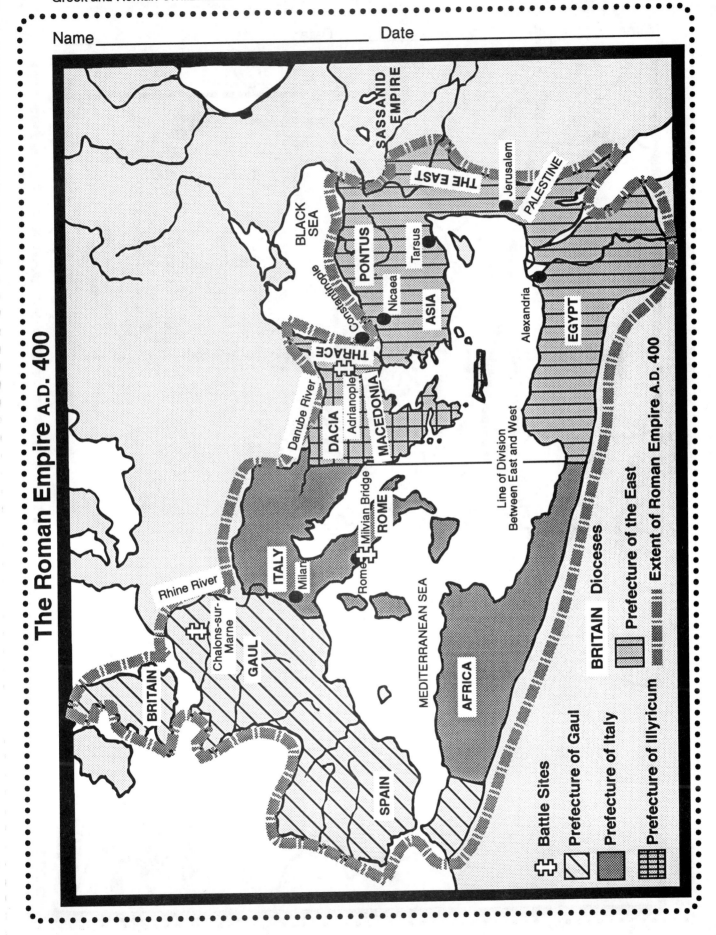

The Roman Empire A.D. 400

SASSANID EMPIRE

THE EAST

Jerusalem

PALESTINE

BLACK SEA

PONTUS

Tarsus

Constantinople

Nicaea

ASIA

Alexandria

EGYPT

THRACE

Adrianople

MACEDONIA

Danube River

DACIA

Line of Division Between East and West

Milvian Bridge

ROME

Rome

ITALY

Milan

Rhine River

MEDITERRANEAN SEA

Chalons-sur-Marne

GAUL

BRITAIN

AFRICA

SPAIN

The Roman Empire A.D. 400

Battle Sites

BRITAIN Dioceses

Prefecture of Gaul

Prefecture of the East

Prefecture of Italy

Prefecture of Illyricum

Extent of Roman Empire A.D. 400

Name_____ Date_____

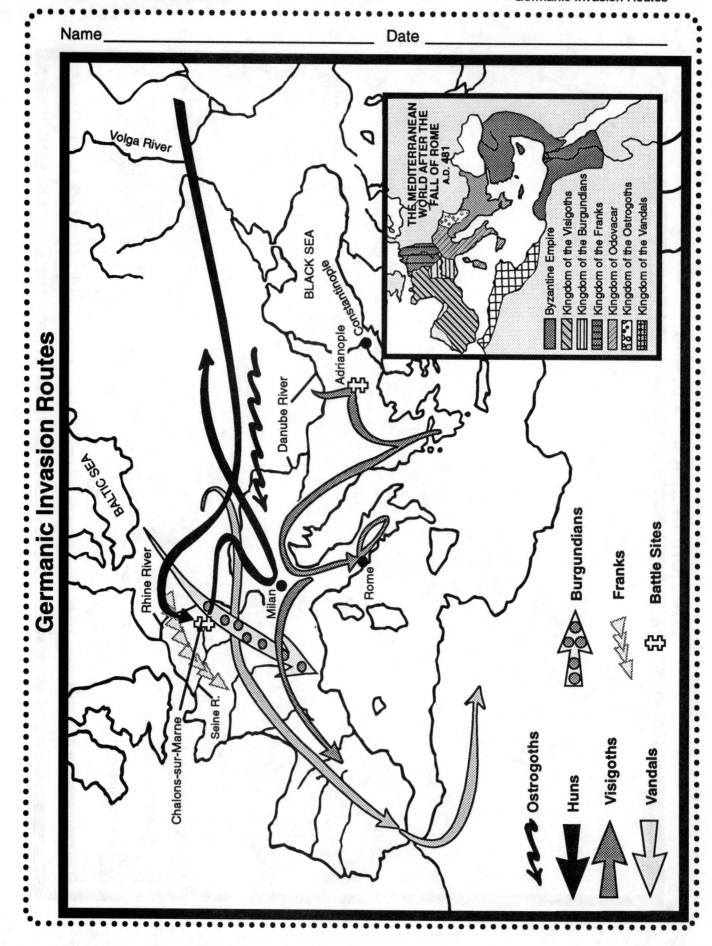

Germanic Invasion Routes

THE MEDITERRANEAN WORLD AFTER THE FALL OF ROME A.D. 481

Byzantine Empire
Kingdom of the Visigoths
Kingdom of the Burgundians
Kingdom of the Franks
Kingdom of Odovacar
Kingdom of the Ostrogoths
Kingdom of the Vandals

Volga River

BALTIC SEA

BLACK SEA

Danube River

Adrianople

Constantinople

Rhine River

Seine R.

Chalons-sur-Marne

Milan

Rome

Burgundians

Franks

Battle Sites

Ostrogoths

Huns

Visigoths

Vandals

Name _____ Date _____

GREEK AND ROMAN MAP ACTIVITY

Locate the following places or areas on the map below by placing the number of the item on the corresponding line on the map.

Greek Civilization

1. Athens
2. Sparta
3. Knossos
4. Mycenae
5. Macedonia
6. Ionia
7. Troy
8. Crete
9. Euphrates River
10. Alexandria
11. Marathon (battle)
12. Thermopylae (battle)
13. Babylon

Roman Civilization

14. Rome
15. Rhine River
16. Danube River
17. Sicily
18. Cannae (battle)
19. Actium (battle)
20. Carthage
21. Constantinople
22. Gaul
23. Zama (battle)
24. Adrianople (battle)
25. Britain

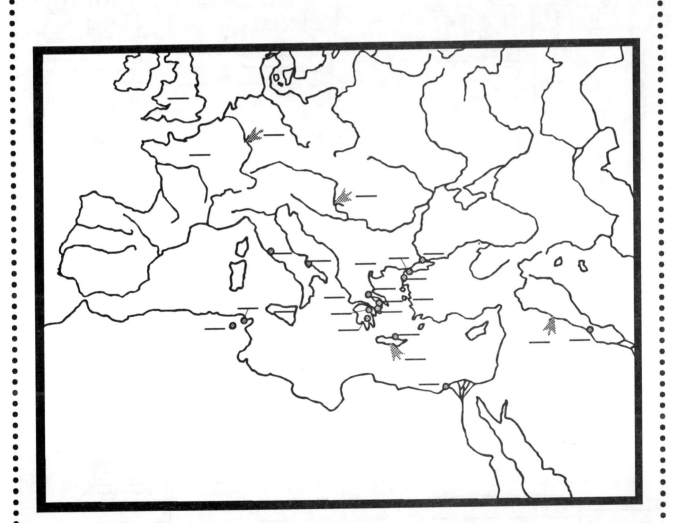

Name _____   Date _____

IDENTIFYING THE PARTS OF A GREEK TEMPLE

Identify the architectural orders and the different parts of a Greek temple. Write in the correct terms on the lines next to the parts or make a numbered list on a sheet of paper.

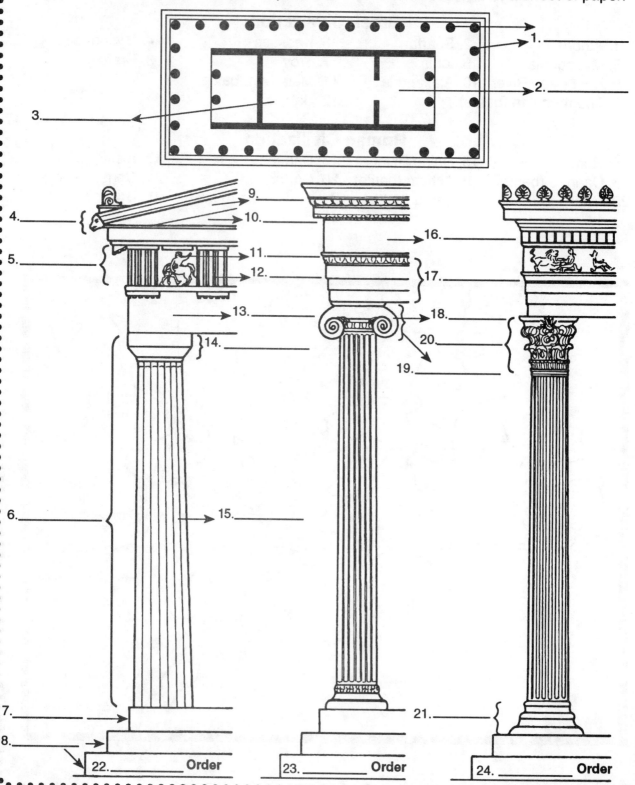

1. _____
2. _____
3. _____
4. _____
5. _____
6. _____
7. _____
8. _____
9. _____
10. _____
11. _____
12. _____
13. _____
14. _____
15. _____
16. _____
17. _____
18. _____
19. _____
20. _____
21. _____
22. _____ Order
23. _____ Order
24. _____ Order

Name _____ Date _____

GREEK HISTORY CROSSWORD

Use the clues below to fill in the crossword puzzle.

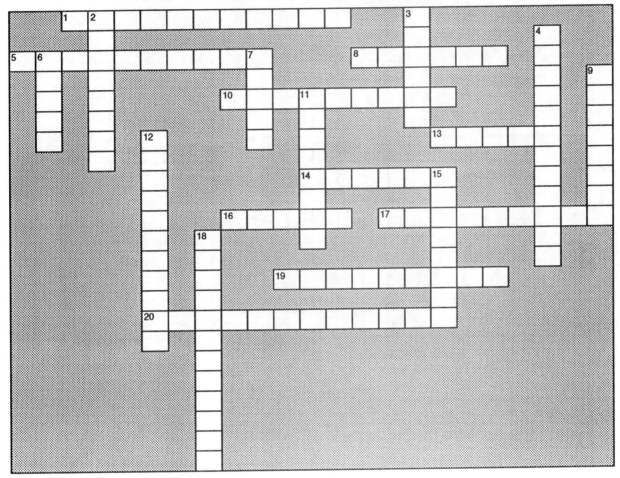

ACROSS

1. Athenian leader who redivided the Athenians into ten new tribes and instituted ostracism
5. He wrote the history of the Peloponnesian War.
8. First Persian king to invade Greece during the Persian Wars
10. Macedonian king who conquered the Persians
13. First king of the Persian empire
14. Macedonian king who conquered the Greeks
16. Legendary king of Crete
17. He wrote about the Persian Wars.
19. Fifth century B.C. tragedian who wrote *Oedipus the King*
20. Fifth century B.C. comic playwrite who mocked his contemporaries

DOWN

2. He instituted the Spartan military educational system.
3. Second Persian king to invade Greece during the Persian Wars
4. Athenian tyrant who embellished Athens with monuments
6. He wrote about the heroic deeds of kings of the Mycenaean period and the Trojan War.
7. Athenian leader who started the wheels of democracy in Greece
9. Spartan general who was killed in the Battle of Thermopylae
11. He wrote the history of Greece during the fourth century B.C.
12. Theban leader who made the city of Thebes a great power during the fourth century B.C.
15. Greatest statesman of Athens who made the city the power of Greece during the fifth century B.C.
18. Great Athenian general during the Persian Wars who created the Athenian navy

95

ROMAN HISTORY CROSSWORD

Name _____ Date _____

Use the clues below to complete the crossword puzzle.

ACROSS

1. Set up the tetrarchy and issued an edict of prices
4. Dictator of the Roman Republic after the first civil war
5. Carthaginian general during the Second Punic War
7. During his reign, the Great Fire of Rome occurred.
8. Fought Mark Antony in the Battle of Actium
11. Made the army the backbone of Imperial power
12. First king of Rome
15. Leader of the Huns
16. During his reign, Mount Vesuvius erupted.
18. First emperor of the Roman Empire
20. Fought Julius Caesar in the second civil war of the Republic
21. Emperor who conquered Britain
22. Started the construction of the Colosseum

DOWN

2. The greatest extent of the Roman Empire was reached during his reign.
3. He succeeded Augustus as emperor.
6. Founded Constantinople as the new capital of the Roman Empire
9. Conquered Gaul
10. He was known as the philosopher-king.
13. Leader of the slave revolt in southern Italy during the first century B.C.
14. Created the Roman professional army
17. He built the defensive wall in Britain that was named after him.
19. Made Christianity the official religion of the Roman Empire
20. Greek general who fought the Romans in southern Italy during the early Republic

THE MATCHING GAME

Match these people, places, and events in Greek and Roman history by placing the letter of the item in Column B on the line next to the corresponding term in Column A. There is only one answer for each term.

COLUMN A	COLUMN B
_____ 1. Alexander the Great	A. Main palace of the Minoan civilization
_____ 2. Attila	B. Aristocracy
_____ 3. Battle of Actium	C. War between Athens and Sparta
_____ 4. Battle of Cannae	D. Listed the accomplishments of Augustus
_____ 5. Battle of Marathon	E. Voting with pot shards to exile someone
_____ 6. Byzantine Empire	F. Roman Peace
_____ 7. Colosseum	G. First Christian emperor
_____ 8. Constantine the Great	H. Metal used more in the Dark Age
_____ 9. Democracy	I. Author of the *Iliad*
_____ 10. Etruscans	J. Rule by four people
_____ 11. Forum	K. Roman Empire in the east
_____ 12. Herodotus	L. Battle site of greatest victory for Hannibal of Carthage
_____ 13. Hippodrome	M. King of the Greeks and Persians
_____ 14. Homer	N. Rule by the people
_____ 15. Iron	O. Darius was defeated by the Greeks in this battle
_____ 16. Julius Caesar	P. The Olympic Games were in honor of this god
_____ 17. Knossos	Q. Greek historian who told of the Persian Wars
_____ 18. Oligarchy	R. City-state that controlled most of the Peloponnese
_____ 19. Ostracism	S. Greek word for city-state
_____ 20. Patricians	T. Octavian defeated Antony and Cleopatra in this battle
_____ 21. Pax Romana	U. Rule by the few
_____ 22. Peloponnesian War	V. Gladiator fights were held here
_____ 23. Pericles	W. Leader of the Huns
_____ 24. Persians	X. Athens' greatest leader
_____ 25. Plebeians	Y. Stadium for equestrian events
_____ 26. Polis	Z. Romans adopted the arch from these people
_____ 27. Res Gestae	AA. The common people of Rome
_____ 28. Sparta	AB. Social and commercial center of a Roman city
_____ 29. Tetrarchy	AC. Xerxes was the king of these people
_____ 30. Zeus	AD. Led the Romans in the Gallic Wars

ANSWERS TO CHALLENGES

Knossos (page 3)
1. Arthur Evans in about 1900
2. King Minos of the labyrinth
3. half-man, half-bull mythological monster; ate people
4. son of the King of Athens; freed Athens from sending people to Crete
5. island of Crete
6. Knossos
7. boxing and bull-leaping
8. Egypt and the Near East
9. royal residence; storage and distribution of goods; daily business of the land was carried out
10. pottery, stone vessels, jewelry

Mycenae (page 6)
1. Greeks
2. wooden horse
3. Homer
4. Heinrich Schliemann
5. Peloponnese on mainland Greece
6. Linear B
7. civil war, drought, invasion
8. olives and grapes
9. pottery, jewelry, weapons, and arms
10. underground tunnels leading to a water well
11. chamber dug into a hillside approached by a long entrance

The Rise of Hellenic Civilization (page 10)
1. development of trade; introduction of the alphabet; emergence of the city-state
2. the use of iron for tools and weapons
3. Greek migration across the Aegean Sea (Ionian Migration)
4. Dorians, Ionians, Aeolians
5. Athens, Sparta, Thebes
6. on the coasts of the Black Sea and northern Aegean Sea, southern Italy and Sicily, and the coasts of France and Spain
7. Eretria and Chalkis, Corinth, Athens, Miletus, and Phocaea
8. the middle class or merchants
9. tyrant of Athens in the fifth century B.C.
10. Massalia, Phaestum and Cumae, Syracuse, Byzantium
11. rule by a king
12. rule by a few wealthy men or families

Lycurgus and Sparta (page 13)
1. semi-legendary lawmaker of Sparta
2. produce men of military strength and loyal soldiers
3. Lycurgus
4. war captives of Sparta; were made slaves
5. war captives of Sparta; were freedmen but socially

inferior to the Spartiates
6. citizens from Sparta
7. the ephors
8. advising the ephors
9. generals of the army
10. to veto or approve any proposal of the state

Athens and Democracy (page 16)
1. rule of the demos or people
2. Athens
3. Solon, Peisistratus, Cleisthenes, Pericles
4. Meetings were held on a hill called the Areopagus.
5. exile for ten years of men who threatened the city-state
6. archons
7. American government
8. Cleisthenes
9. Solon
10. people: not enough power given; aristocracy: power taken away from them

The Wars with Persia (page 20)
1. Cyrus the Great
2. Cyrus the Great; Cambyses, Darius
3. west-east: the Mediterranean coast to the Indus River; north-south: Black Sea to the Persian Gulf
4. province of Persia
5. effective communication system: the Royal Road
6. Persepolis
7. Ionian Revolt
8. Herodotus
9. Battle of Thermopylae
10. Greek warship
11. King Darius
12. King Xerxes
13. expansion into Europe; revenge upon Athens

The Peloponnesian War and Its Aftermath (page 24)
1. Sparta and Athens
2. Pericles
3. confederation of Athens and mainly Asiatic Greek city-states; Athens was the leader
4. to protect and liberate the Asiatic and other Greek city-states from Persian control
5. Thucidides
6. Sparta
7. Battle of Aegospotami
8. a skilled general who ruled Thebes for a short period before 362 B.C.
9. King of Macedonia
10. Battle of Chaeronea

Alexander the Great (page 27)

1. King of Macedonia; son of Philip II
2. Darius III
3. Babylon
4. Battle of Gaugamela
5. 331 B.C.
6. Alexandria
7. Indus River
8. his army revolted
9. Arrian; *Anabasis*
10. malaria or poisoning

Greek Art and Architecture (page 32)

1. Acropolis; Agora
2. Parthenon
3. the temple
4. house the statue of the patron-god or goddess; keep offerings
5. the naos
6. Doric, Ionic, Corinthian
7. Pheidias
8. the columns: plain (Doric); volute with egg-and-dart pattern (Ionic); acanthus leaves growing from the shaft (Corinthian)
9. Black Figure and Red Figure Pottery
10. temples, houses, public buildings, along the streets

Theater and Games (page 36)

1. It was a religious and social event held in honor of a god.
2. tragedies and comedies
3. Aeschylus, Sophocles, and Euripides
4. a comic poet
5. A chorus danced and sang, commenting on the events in the play.
6. Zeus, the king of the gods
7. stadium where equestrian events were held
8. Olympic Games
9. chariot race, horse race, boxing, wrestling, pancration, pentathlon, track races, race in armor
10. orchestra, seating area, stage building
11. *Oedipus the King*
12. *The Persians*

The Etruscans and the Beginning of Rome (page 40)

1. Italians, Greeks, Etruscans
2. Etruria, between the Tiber and Arno Rivers
3. bronze work
4. founder and first king of Rome
5. in carved sarcophaghi or urns placed in rock-cut chamber tombs
6. a she-wolf and, later, a shepherd
7. arch, alphabet, reading into the future, art of bronze making, and aspects of the government

8. Latin
9. architecture, sculpture, science, and literature
10. 12 independent city-states, each ruled by a king
11. Tiber River

The Republic of Rome Part 1: 509–218 B.C. (page 44)

1. advisory body to the consuls
2. executive leaders of Rome
3. wealthy land-owning aristocracy
4. common people
5. a law in which the People's Assembly was officially recognized and had the force of law
6. Sardinia and Sicily combined
7. Greek general who helped the Greeks in southern Italy fight the Romans
8. Punic is latin for Phoenician; the people from Carthage were Phoenicians.
9. consul, city judge, public relations officer, financial officer, high priest
10. conquered territory that had to supply taxes to the Romans

The Republic of Rome Part 2: Hannibal 218–133 B.C. (page 47)

1. Carthaginian general
2. Roman general; fought Hannibal of Carthage
3. Hannibal's
4. Battle of Cannae, 206 B.C.
5. Battle of Zama, 202 B.C.
6. two provinces of Spain
7. 7; 3
8. Africa and Macedonia-Greece
9. Second Punic War
10. Third Punic War
11. It was left to the Romans upon the death of King Attalus of Pergamon.

The Republic of Rome Part 3: Civil Wars 133–46 B.C. (page 51)

1. social reformers of Rome
2. to reinstall the small landholders and take care of urban poverty
3. formation of a professional Roman army
4. Roman general who, after a civil war, became dictator of Rome.
5. Pompey and Caesar
6. Roman general and leader of Rome
7. slave who led a rebellion in southern Italy
8. a political coalition between Pompey, Crassus, and Caesar; all three men shared the power in Rome
9. Battle of Pharsalus, 48 B.C.
10. ambition of the Roman leaders
11. plebeians versus the patricians (commoners vs. rulers)

The Republic of Rome Part 4: Julius Caesar (page 54)

1. Roman military leader who became dictator of Rome
2. Gaul
3. The Gauls posed a threat to the nearby provinces of Rome.
4. Caesar's ambition and desire for military prestige
5. Pompey
6. Cleopatra
7. Roman calendar
8. Cassius and Brutus and other Senate conspirators
9. Ides of March (March 15) 44 B.C.
10. new settlement for war veterans and the poor; place of defense; instrument of Romanization of the provinces

Octavian-Augustus: The First Roman Emperor (page 58)

1. Battles at Philippi
2. Augustus
3. Octavian and Antony
4. Battle of Actium
5. written testament of Augustus's life and achievements as emperor of Rome
6. Roman Peace
7. Tiberius, Augustus's stepson
8. He restored the Republic.
9. end of the Roman Republic; Octavian became master of the Graeco-Roman world; the Roman state was dominated by the West with the capital in Rome
10. Rhine and Danube Rivers

Notable Emperors: The Early Roman Empire A.D. 14–180 (page 62)

1. Claudius
2. the Christians
3. Nero's reign
4. Mount Vesuvius, near Naples
5. Trajan's reign
6. Hadrian
7. Dacia, Armenia, Mesopotamia, and part of Arabia
8. Marcus Aurelius
9. It was lavishly decorated with gold.
10. Trajan's achievements and victories in Dacia

Notable Emperors: The Late Roman Empire A.D. 180–305 (page 66)

1. 50-year period of civil war; many emperors claimed to rule the empire at the same time
2. Septimius Severus
3. son of Marcus Aurelius; Rome's most eccentric emperor
4. Diocletian
5. Rule of four people; two co-emperors and two Caesars
6. diocese and prefecture
7. edict that fixed the maximum prices on all goods and set maximum wages for workers
8. get along and care only for the soldiers
9. non-existent; the sharing of power was gone
10. He divided the army into two branches: a mobile field force and a frontier force.

The Rise and Spread of Christianity (page 70)

1. province of Judaea, Palestine
2. belief in many gods
3. paganism
4. edict legalizing Christianity in the eastern half of the Roman Empire, A.D. 311
5. Constantine the Great
6. Theodosius the Great
7. Edict of Milan
8. Egyptian priest who founded Arianism
9. a movement within Christianity that stated the three individuals of the Trinity were not equal; regarded as a heresy
10. Battle of the Milvian Bridge, Rome

The Fall of the Roman Empire A.D. 337–476 (page 74)

1. Battle of Adrianople
2. western movement of the Huns
3. Battle at Chalons on the Marne River
4. fierce leader of the Huns
5. It started the massive Germanic invasions across the Rhine frontier; it showed the Germans that the Roman army was not invincible.
6. Franks, Burgundians, Vandals, Visigoths
7. Romulus Augustulus
8. the German general Odovacar
9. Byzantine Empire
10. Battle of Adrianople

Roman Architecture (page 79)

1. the central public marketplace of a Roman city
2. the transportation of water to a city
3. the arch
4. a cement made of volcanic dust and lime mortar
5. a temple dedicated to all gods, built by Hadrian
6. the Classical orders of the Greek temple, most commonly the Corinthian order
7. the atrium or living room
8. Arches are crossed in different directions in a circular space and intersect at the center.
9. a series of arches side by side
10. a pool in the center of the atrium that collects rainwater

Entertainment (page 82)

1. amphitheater where public events, such as mock sea battles and gladiatorial fight were held
2. Circus Maximus
3. Colosseum
4. The wounded gladiator was to be killed.
5. "We who are about to die salute you."
6. by being thrown unarmed to wild lions and bears
7. part of a religious ritual, as blood sacrifices, in Etruscans festivals
8. an underground heating system to heat the waters of a Roman bath
9. oil and a strigil for scraping off the dirt and oil
10. cold, warm, hot, and dry sweating baths

The Roman Army (page 86)

1. legion
2. century
3. Marius
4. a unit of the Roman army; made up of six centuries
5. the chief commander of all the legions; the emperor during the Imperial period
6. the auxiliary army units: the cavalry and light-armed troops
7. metal body armor over a linen vest, which was worn over a woolen tunic; cloak; hobnailed sandals; shield; and helmet
8. Roman siege machine; catapult that hurled stones and flaring darts
9. a permanent Roman camp for soldiers along the frontiers
10. writers, accountants, engineers, surveyors, and carpenters

ANSWERS TO ACTIVITIES

Roman Numeral Activity (page ix)

1. 88
2. 2009
3. 702
4. 661
5. 930
6. 18
7. 44
8. 373
9. 456
10. 89

Greek and Roman Map Activity (page 93)

See various maps for correct locations.

Identifying the Parts of a Greek Temple (page 94)

1. colonnade or peristyle
2. pronaos
3. cella or naos
4. cornice
5. frieze
6. column
7. stylobate
8. stereobate
9. geison
10. pediment
11. metope
12. triglyph
13. architrave
14. capital
15. shaft
16. frieze
17. architrave
18. volute
19. capital
20. capital
21. base
22. Doric Order
23. Ionic Order
24. Corinthian Order

Greek History Crossword (page 95)

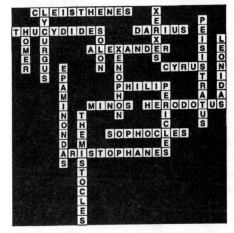

Roman History Crossword (page 96)

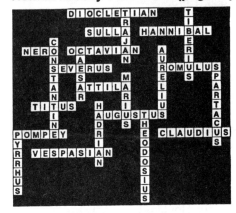

The Matching Game (page 97)

1. M
2. W
3. T
4. L
5. O
6. K
7. V
8. G
9. N
10. Z
11. AB
12. Q
13. Y
14. I
15. H
16. AD
17. A
18. U
19. E
20. B
21. F
22. C
23. X
24. AC
25. AA
26. S
27. D
28. R
29. J
30. P

SELECTED REFERENCES

Greek History
Primary Sources
Arrian. *The Campaigns of Alexander.* New York: Penguin Books, 1976.

Herodotus. *The Histories.* New York: Penguin Books, 1983.

Homer. *The Iliad.* New York: Penguin Books, 1988.

Homer. *The Odyssey.* New York: Penguin Books, 1982.

Thucydides. *The Peloponnesian War.* New York: Penguin Books, 1980.

Xenophon. *A History of My Times.* New York: Penguin Books, 1981.

Secondary Sources
Amos, Hugh Desmond. *These Were the Greeks.* Chester Springs, Pennsylvania: Dufour Editions Inc., 1992.

Boardman, John. *The Greeks Overseas.* London: Thames and Hudson, 1988.

Boardman, John. *Greek Art.* New York: Thames and Hudson, 1985.

Burn, Andrew Robert. *Persia and the Greeks: The Defense of the West.* London: Stanford University Press, 1984.

Burn, Andrew Robert. *The Penquin History of Greece.* New York: Penguin Books, 1990.

Davies, John Kenyon. *Democracy and Classical Greece.* Cambridge, Massachusetts: Harvard University Press, 1993.

Dickinson, Oliver. *The Aegean Bronze Age.* Cambridge, U.K.: Cambridge University Press, 1994.

Dinsmoor, William Bell. *The Architecture of Greece.* New York: W.W. Norton and Co., 1975.

Ellis, John. *Philip II and Macedonian Imperialism.* Princeton, New Jersey: Princeton University Press, 1986.

Finley, Moses. *The Ancient Greeks.* New York: Penguin Books, 1987.

Huxley, George Leonard. *Early Sparta.* Cambridge, Massachusetts: Harvard University Press, 1962.

Jones, Arnold Hugh Martin. *Athenian Democracy.* Baltimore: John Hopkins University Press, 1986.

Kitto, Humphrey Dauy Findley. *The Greeks.* Magnolia, Massachusetts: Peter Smith, 1988.

Marinatos, Spyros. *Crete and Mycenae.* London: Thames and Hudson, 1960.

Meiggs, Russel. *The Athenian Empire.* Oxford, U.K.: Oxford University Press, 1979.

Snodgrass, Anthony. *The Dark Age of Greece.* Edinburgh, U.K.: Edinburgh University Press, 1971.

Wilcken, Ulrich. *Alexander the Great.* New York: W.W. Norton and Co., 1967.

Roman History
Primary Sources
Brunt, P. A. and J. M. Moore, eds. *Res Gestae Divi Augusti* [The Achievements of the Divine Augustus]. Oxford, U.K.: Oxford University Press, 1979.

Julius Caesar. *The Conquest of Gaul.* New York: Penguin Books, 1983.

Livy. *The History of Rome* 14 vols. Cambridge, Massachusetts: Loeb Classics Library, Harvard University Press.

Tacitus. *The Histories.* New York: Penguin Books, 1964.

Tacitus. *The Annals of Imperial Rome.* New York, Penguin Books, 1956.

Secondary Sources
Barrow, Reginald Haynes. *The Romans.* New York: Penguin Books, 1975.

Bunson, Matthew. *Encyclopedia of the Roman Empire.* New York: Facts on File, 1994.

Cambridge Ancient History, vols 7–12. Cambridge, U.K.: Cambridge University Press.

Crawford, Michael. *The Roman Republic.* Cambridge, Massachusetts: Harvard University Press, 1993.

Grant, Michael. *The Fall of the Roman Empire.* New York: MacMillan, 1990.

Grant, Michael. *History of Rome.* New York: MacMillan, 1978.

Grant, Michael. *Gladiators.* London: Weidenfeld and Nicolson, 1971.

Jones, Arnold Hugh Martin. *The Later Roman Empire.* Norman, Oklahoma: University of Oklahoma Press, 1964.

Pallottino, Massimo. *The Etruscans.* New York: Penquin Books, 1978.

Watson, George Ronald. *The Roman Soldier.* Ithaca, New York: Cornell University Press, 1985.

Webster, Graham. *The Roman Imperial Army.* New York: Barnes and Noble, 1994.

Wheeler, Mortimer. *Roman Art and Architecture.* New York: Thames and Hudson, 1985.

Wilkes, John. *The Roman Army.* Cambridge, U.K.: Cambridge University Press, 1986.